A Guide to Keynes

Alvin H. Hansen

LUCIUS N. LITTAUER PROFESSOR OF POLITICAL ECONOMY
HARVARD UNIVERSITY

New York   Toronto   London

McGRAW-HILL BOOK COMPANY, INC.

1953

A GUIDE TO KEYNES

Library of Congress Catalog Card Number: 52–13006

VII

THE MAPLE PRESS COMPANY, YORK, PA.

Preface

This book is intended primarily for students majoring in economics and for first-year graduate students. Its aim is to assist, and induce, the student to read the *General Theory*.[1] Too often nowadays the student reads a good deal of the literature *about* Keynes but little in the *General Theory* itself.

It is my experience that very many students find the *General Theory* a difficult book. It is the purpose of this volume to serve, so to speak, as a tutorial guide. The student is advised to read and reread the relevant sections in the *General Theory* in conjunction with the present volume.

There is available, by now, a number of books which offer the student a "short cut" to Keynes. The present volume does not belong to this category. It is not a substitute for Keynes. The short cuts are not likely to help the student to read the difficult parts in the *General Theory*. By attempting to "make Keynes easy" they are indeed likely to leave the student, quite unintentionally no doubt, with wrong ideas about what Keynes really said.

I have tried in this volume to face the difficult parts in the *General Theory* head on. And especially I have tried to underscore precisely what Keynes said on controversial issues. In considerable measure (but not always) the controversy vanishes once it becomes clear what Keynes *did* say.

No one can reread Keynes without being impressed with the fact that he succeeded, to an astonishing degree, in

[1] Throughout this volume the commonly used shorter title, *The General Theory*, is used instead of the full title of Keynes's great work, *The General Theory of Employment, Interest and Money*, Harcourt, Brace and Company, Inc., 1936.

v

anticipating his critics. But he was not always right, and where this is the case I have endeavored to point it out. On the other hand, I have set phrases, which taken by themselves alone are likely to be misinterpreted, against the larger background of the book as a whole. A debater may look for points, but scholarship demands that we take a look at the whole.

No doubt practiced readers will find, here and there, that I am quite wrong in what I say. It would be foolish to claim the final word on so difficult a subject, and I have no illusions on that score. But throughout this volume I have constantly tried to cite chapter and verse so that the reader who may question my interpretation of any particular point can readily refer back to Keynes himself.

I wish to express my appreciation for the facilities for research made available by the Graduate School of Public Administration of Harvard University and for stimulating discussions with graduate students and colleagues in the Department of Economics. I am indebted to Dr. Richard Goodwin for helpful suggestions; to Professor Paul Samuelson and Professor Abba Lerner for comments on the chapter on interest-rate theory. None of them is to be held responsible, however, for what I have written. I am also grateful to Mrs. Berwyn Fragner and Mrs. Robert Lindsay for assistance in preparing the manuscript for the printer and to Mrs. Lindsay for making the index.

I wish to express appreciation for permission to quote generously, which permissions have been granted by the authors and publishers and are duly noted in the footnote references. My thanks are especially due, in view of the exceptionally large number of quotations from *The General Theory*, to the Keynes trustees and Harcourt, Brace and Company, Inc.

Alvin H. Hansen

CAMBRIDGE, MASS.

FEBRUARY, 1953

Contents

Editor's Introduction

For years many teachers of economics and other professional economists have felt the need of a series of books on economic subjects which is not filled by the usual textbook or by the highly technical treatise.

This present series, published under the general title, the Economics Handbook Series, was planned with these needs in mind. Designed first of all for students, the volumes are useful in the ever-growing field of adult education and also are of interest to the informed general reader.

The volumes are not long—they give the essentials of the subject matter within the limits of a few hundred pages; they present a distillate of accepted theory and practice, without the detailed approach of the technical treatise. Each volume is a unit, standing on its own.

The authors are scholars, each writing on an economic subject on which he is an authority. In this series the author's first task was not to make important contributions to knowledge—although many of them do—but so to present his subject matter that his work as a scholar will carry its maximum influence outside as well as inside the classroom. The time has come to redress the balance between the energies spent on the creation of new ideas and on their dissemination. Economic ideas are unproductive if they do not spread beyond the world of scholars. Popularizers without technical competence, unqualified textbook writers, and sometimes even charlatans, control too large a part of the market for economic ideas.

In the classroom the Economics Handbook Series will serve, it is hoped, as brief surveys in one-semester courses, as supplementary reading in introductory courses, and in other courses in which the subject is related.

In 1936, Keynes published his famous *General Theory of Employment, Interest and Money*. There are few who would deny, as of now, seventeen years later, that the book has had a greater impact on economic analysis and policy even in this short time than any book since Ricardo's *Political Economy*. It may be a little too early to claim that, along with Darwin's *Origin of Species* and Karl Marx's *Das Capital*, the *General Theory* is one of the most significant books which have appeared in the last hundred years. (Darwin's book, though not strictly in the social sciences, greatly affected them.) But whatever the exact significance of the *General Theory*—and the results of the ideological struggle of our age will influence the long-run assessment—it is clear, judging from the reviews of the book when it first came out, that it has had a much greater effect than most had anticipated in 1936. It continues to gain in importance. Not surprising is the fact that few aside from Keynes's closest "collaborators" came even near to sensing the place the *General Theory* was to occupy in economics. Keynes, however, had once boasted in a letter to G. B. Shaw, of his forthcoming revolutionary book, the *General Theory*.

Breaking new ground, Keynes encountered all kinds of difficulties. The fact that he wrote the book in his fifties, a well-advanced age for highly creative work, together with the great demands made upon him by his richly diversified activities, may partly account for the deficiencies of the book. These certainly help to explain his failure to read more widely as well as to some extent his originality—for the less versed in what others write, the easier a fresh approach. The exposition proved difficult; many ideas had not been clearly thought out; there were some confusions and even errors; the relation of the *General Theory* to the accepted doctrine was not at all clear; and Keynes, like many other innovators, and particularly those not immersed in the literature, was inclined to exaggerate the novelty of his approach and development. Those conversant with Keynes's *Economic Consequences of Peace*, his *Tract on Monetary Reform*, his *Essays in Persuasion*, and the many brilliantly written parts of the *Treatise on Money* were disappointed in the writing, which seemed not up to Keynes's usually sparkling literary skill.

Few books as difficult to read (*Das Kapital*, about which Keynes complained as a confused work, is a somewhat similar case) have had anything like the wide success of the *General Theory*. This success reflects intrinsic merit, for few books have had the fine combing both by believers and by vigorous critics.

Unfortunately, Keynes had little opportunity or leisure to clarify his views in his last decade following the publication of the *General Theory*. The international crisis required virtually all his energies in those years; and a serious illness limited his working day. At least, his *How to Pay for the War* (1940) cleared up one point: that his system applied to inflationary as well as deflationary periods. Keynes had some brilliant students at Cambridge, and they, other followers, and other economists in the years after 1936, and Keynes himself to some extent, cleared up obscurities, improved the integration of the various parts, and eliminated positive error. This naturally helped to put Keynes in perspective.[1]

Professor Hansen is the obvious choice for a volume on Keynes in the Economics Handbook Series. As the most prominent Keynesian in the United States, Hansen has interpreted Keynesian economics for American students and laymen; and he has greatly enriched it as well.

In writing *A Guide to Keynes*, Professor Hansen expresses the hope that the student or informed layman will continue to

[1] See *The New Economics*, edited with an introduction by Seymour E. Harris, Alfred A. Knopf, Inc., 1947, especially Parts 1–3, 9.

read the *General Theory*. Sweating through a 400-page classic like the *General Theory* is part of the educational process. The professional economist who has not given a summer to a thorough study of Keynes's *General Theory* has lost much.

But there are many who can spare but a few days or a week or two or three on Keynes. This applies to many undergraduates who must learn about Keynes's work as part of a single course in economics, or even to students who devote several courses to economics, and to the numerous laymen who may want to know what Keynes is about. Even those who choose the painful though profitable task of reading and interpreting the *General Theory* will be greatly helped on their way by Professor Hansen's new book.

Page by page, line by line, he has culled the fruits of the *General Theory*. He not only has weeded and raked the rich field but also has fertilized the soil and replanted to achieve the landscape envisaged by Keynes.

The resulting product is a rare one which few who wish to understand Keynes and modern economics can afford to neglect. Every page of Professor Hansen's book reflects his painstaking examination of practically every paragraph of the *General Theory*, as well as his command of the literature, both European and American. The book reflects, also, many years of teaching Keynes's theories to students, both graduate and undergraduate, in his courses in business cycles, money and banking, and fiscal policy and the guidance of many theses dealing with Keynesian economics. Hansen's *Guide* also reflects many of his own contributions to the system about which he modestly remains silent (*e.g.*, his treatment of economic maturity, of the consumption function, international disequilibrium, the problems raised by the financing of deficits, the integration of local, state, and Federal finance as facets of full employment policy) and reflects finally the fruits of years of application of Keynesian economics to the policy questions of an economy floundering between deflation and unemployment, on the one hand, and full employment and inflation, on the other.

Space does not allow a listing of all the aspects of Keynesian economics on which Professor Hansen sheds light in this book. Suffice it to present but a few: the validity of Say's law; the relation of the marginal efficiency of capital, the consumption function, and the rate of interest to the level of employment; relation of savings and investment; the appraisal of the static, periodic, and dynamic aspects of Keynes's theory; the three versions of the multiplier; the own rates of interest; the reconciliation of Keynes's liquidity theory of interest, the loan fund, and the Hicksian theory; the relation of effective demand, money, and prices; the assumptions under which Keynes developed his analysis, etc.

ı Hansen is a great admirer of Keynes; but this does not blind him to credit or discredit where it is due. For instance, he is critical of Keynes for his failure to give the Continental economists and many of the English economists, particularly Professor D. H. Robertson and Professor Pigou, adequate credit for their contributions. When Keynes claims too much, Hansen gently reminds the reader of Keynes's overreaching. Errors, confusions, inconsistencies, failure to carry a line of reasoning through, irresponsible statements—all these receive the attention of Keynes's friendly but firm critic. But more important, Professor Hansen measures Keynes's unprecedented contributions to economics. ı

My prediction is that the net result of Professor Hansen's book will be a much wider understanding of Keynes's economics and Keynesian economics. and that it will result in the *General Theory* being read more than ever.

Seymour E. Harris

NOTE ON PAGE REFERENCES,
TERMINOLOGY, AND NOMENCLATURE

At the head of each chapter in this volume, reference is made to the chapter or chapters in the *General Theory* which are under discussion. Scattered throughout each chapter, I have made page references to the *General Theory*. All page references, unless otherwise indicated, are to the *General Theory*.

Frequently, I have grouped two or more of Keynes's chapters for treatment under one general heading. Accordingly, this volume contains only thirteen chapters, while the *General Theory* contains twenty-four.

I have, however, followed in general the sequence of topics found in Keynes's book. A more logical arrangement might indeed be offered, but any drastic rearrangement would have defeated my primary purpose; namely, to induce the student to read, and help him to understand Keynes. The *General Theory* and the present volume can therefore conveniently be read side by side.

For the most part, I have followed Keynes's terminology and nomenclature. There are, however, the following exceptions, which the student should carefully note:

1. Marginal efficiency of capital. For this I use the symbol r; Keynes uses no symbol for this concept.
2. Rate of interest. For this I use the symbol i; Keynes uses the symbol r.
3. Liquidity preference functions:
   a. Total liquidity preference function (including both the transactions demand and the asset demand for money). This function I write as follows: $L = L(Y,i)$; Keynes's nomenclature is $M = L(Y,r)$.
   b. Transactions-demand function. I write it as follows: $L' = L'(Y)$; Keynes writes it $M_1 = L_1(Y)$.
   c. Asset-demand function. I write it as follows: $L'' = L''(i)$; Keynes writes it $M_2 = L_2(r)$.

Book One

Introduction

CHAPTER 1

The Postulates of the Classical Economics
and the Principle of Effective Demand

[GENERAL THEORY, CHAPTERS 1–3]

PRE-KEYNESIAN DISSENTERS

It is safe to say that any economic doctrine long accepted by any considerable group of competent economists was never wholly without merit. Though later discarded, such doctrines often afforded as a first approximation significant insights into the functioning of the economic system. This is true, for example, of the long-since-discredited wages-fund theory, and it is true of Say's law. In both cases (under the stress of petty and often sterile controversy) rigid and dogmatic formulations emerged—stereotyped "laws" which sought to compress very complex phenomena into a rigid mold. But in flexible hands, and for those with fluid minds, these theories could be—and often were—illuminating and useful.

Say's law, in a very broad way, is a description of a free-exchange economy. So conceived, it illuminates the truth that the main source of demand is the flow of factor income generated from the process of production itself. The employment of hitherto unused resources, by adding to the circular flow of income and output, pays its own way since it enlarges the income stream by an amount equivalent (in equilibrium conditions) to the amount taken out of the income stream through the sale of its products. A new productive process, by paying out income to its employed factors, generates demand at the same time that it adds to supply.

3

The classic statement of Say's law maintained the thesis that the free-price system tends to provide a place for a growing population and an increase in capital. In an expanding society, new firms and new workers wedge their way into the productive process, not by supplanting others, but by offering their own products in exchange. The market is not regarded as fixed or limited—incapable of expansion. The market is as big as the volume of products offered in exchange. Supply creates its own demand. Viewed as a broad generalization, this statement presents in the large a picture of the exchange economy.

But the history of thought illustrates again and again how a great, living principle, tossed about on the sea of controversy, is likely to lose its vitality. Too often it may be applied, as a tool of analysis, to highly complex problems for which it is unsuited. Misleading conclusions inevitably emerge. This is what happened to Say's law.

Beginning students who read the current literature on the "Keynesian revolution" are likely to get the impression that all economists, young and old alike, presented up to 1936— the year in which the *General Theory* was published—a solid orthodox-classical front. Nothing could be further from the truth. The generation of economists embarking upon their professional life in the period around the First World War were in no inconsiderable measure unhappy about the then prevailing state of economic analysis. The prevailing theory was neatly logical, but it was often incapable of coming to grips with reality. Many economists, accordingly, turned to descriptive and institutional studies.

This state of distrust of orthodox theory was indeed not peculiar to the period referred to above. On the contrary this situation had been the rule, except for rare intervals, since the days of Ricardo. R. L. Meek, in his article on "The Decline of Ricardian Economics in England,"[1] cites evidence, from the

[1] *Economica*, February, 1950.

proceedings of the Political Economy Club, of the "rapid decline of certain basic Ricardian doctrines." The years 1823 to 1833 saw widespread attacks on Ricardo. Henry Sidgwick, in his *Principles of Political Economy* (1883), quotes Malthus as saying in 1827 (only four years after Ricardo's death) that "the differences of opinion among political economists" have "of late been a frequent subject of complaint."[1]

J. S. Mill attempted to remedy this situation, and for a time his *Principles* (1848) won wide acceptance. Sir James Stephen, in 1861, was able to report "that the conclusions of those who understand the science are accepted and acted on with a degree of confidence which is felt in regard to no other speculations that deal with human affairs."[2] In commenting on the commanding authority of Mill, Sidgwick stated: "The generation whose study of Political Economy commenced about 1860 were for the most part but dimly conscious of the element of stormy controversy from which the subject had so recently emerged."[3] Yet already by 1869 Mill surrendered to the attacks of Longe and Thornton on the wages-fund dogma, and, in 1871, came Jevons's smashing attack on the then prevailing doctrines. Marshall, however, rebuilt a new orthodoxy (*Principles*, 1890) in his synthesis of the Austrian (and Jevonian) approach with that of the classical system.

Still there were plenty of dissenters.[4] In the United States,

---

[1] H. Sidgwick, *The Principles of Political Economy*, 3d ed., Macmillan & Co., Ltd. (London), reprinted 1924, p. 2.

[2] *Ibid.*, p. 3.

[3] *Ibid.*

[4] Keynes was fully aware that, for decades past, economics had not been a settled and peaceful discipline. He himself had been at the forefront of doctrinal controversy. He had over a long period made a frontal attack on one of the most deeply rooted and awe-inspiring pillars of the modern world —the gold standard. In this battle he had been aided by many of his fellow economists, and at long last he had converted the great majority of British men of affairs in government, industry, and finance. With respect to employment theory and policy there remained "deep divergencies of opinion

the institutionalists—Veblen, Commons, Mitchell, and their followers—were highly skeptical of "pure theory." Facts upon facts were piled up—sociological, legal, and statistical—which often seemed to indicate that the conclusions of orthodox theory failed to conform to the real world. Nevertheless these assaults upon orthodox doctrine must be rated as largely unsuccessful. As President Conant has aptly put it: "It takes a new conceptual scheme to cause the abandonment of an old one." Men strive desperately "to modify an old idea to make it accord with new experiments."[1] Facts alone will not destroy a theory.

As a part of this widespread dissatisfaction with the state of economic theory, Say's law in particular was subjected to serious question. But despite numerous attempts, no one succeeded in making a strong theoretical case against the basic premise that the price system tended automatically to produce full employment. Two powerful defenses were invariably erected against anyone who challenged this fundamental conception: (1) that a flexible interest rate would ensure equality between saving and investment at full employment; (2) that in a system of flexible wages and prices, an adequate market would, except for temporary disturbances, be assured.

In the literature of 1900 to 1936, one finds numerous efforts, some important and many hopelessly defective, to challenge the prevailing orthodox theory of automatic adjustment. On balance, these attempts made little impression, and no good purpose would be served to canvass this literature here. In most cases the critic carried a weak theoretical armour. A good orthodox theorist could usually, by rigorous logic, show him

---

between fellow economists." These divergencies had, Keynes believed, "almost destroyed the practical influence of economic theory, and will continue to do so until they are resolved" (General Theory, Preface).

[1] James B. Conant, On Understanding Science, Yale University Press, 1947, pp. 89, 90.

to be wrong. The most valiant effort was made by Hobson. But he failed essentially because his weapons were in fact inadequate for the task.

In France, Aftalion in his "La Réalité des surproductions générales" (1909)[1] openly attacked Say's law. But this part of his theory (though it is now evident that he was on the right track) was laughed out of court by reviewers both in England and America.[2] Attention was concentrated instead on his contributions to the theory of *oscillations per se*, especially the leads which he opened for econometric business-cycle models. What he had to say on Say's law was misunderstood or ignored.

In the United States, the most penetrating critic of economic orthodoxy was J. M. Clark. He was skeptical of the capacity of the economic system to make automatically the adjustments needed to ensure full employment. He doubted that flexibility of prices, wage rates, or interest rates could be relied upon to ensure full use of productive resources.

Unlike Hobson, Clark made no major, over-all attack on Say's law and the theoretical apparatus supporting it. Himself a first-rate neoclassical thinker, he was sympathetic with, continually made use of, and contributed to the prevailing tools of theoretical analysis. But he was conscious of the shortcomings of theory, and he challenged the arrogant complacency of its supporters in the face of pressing and unsolved problems. In his *Economics of Overhead Costs*, he probed deeply into new territory.

In 1934, Clark published his *Strategic Factors in Business Cycles*, and in the same year appeared his Productive Capacity and Effective Demand, a special chapter in the *Report of the Columbia University Commission on Economic Reconstruction*. This chapter is of unusual interest, for it reveals the intellectual mis-

[1] *Revue d'économie politique*, 1909.

[2] See my *Business Cycles and National Income*, W. W. Norton & Co., 1951, Chap. 18.

givings of a highly competent theorist who, however, was not wedded dogmatically to the prevailing orthodoxy. A brief survey of relevant passages from these volumes will disclose the direction and character of his thinking.

In his chapter on Productive Capacity and Effective Demand he raised the problem of whether there exists "a chronic limitation of production owing to limitation of effective demand."[1] To this he gave a nondogmatic and uncertain answer. He rightly asserted that no definitive analysis of this problem had yet been made. He therefore proposed to make a tentative "analysis of the nature of the mechanism by which potential power to produce is transformed into realized production, balanced and activated by an equivalent effective demand for the products turned out."[2]

He began his analysis on the assumption "that it has been reasonably well established that there exists a very considerable margin of unused productive capacity owing to the condition commonly thought of and spoken of as limited effective demand."[3] Yet the economic system had in fact over the last 150 years assimilated great increases in productive power. "This is a basic fact to be placed alongside the proposition that the system has not assimilated its productive power as fast as that power has come into being."[4] Why, he asked, has the system not assimilated all its productive power, and why has it assimilated as much as it has?

Clark posed two hypotheses for consideration, the first having to do with long-run trends and the second with the cycles of boom and depression.

As a practical matter Clark wished first to stabilize the cycle. Until industrial fluctuations have been dealt with "we

---

[1] *Economic Reconstruction*, Columbia University Press, 1934, p. 105.

[2] *Ibid.*

[3] *Ibid.*, p. 106.

[4] *Ibid.*, p. 107.

can hardly test the truth of the first hypothesis."[1] The first hypothesis has to do with "long-run trends" and assumes that there is "some limitation on the increase of purchasing power" or on the rate at which the economic system can make the necessary adjustments[2] so that "this rate falls short of the rate of increase in our powers of production."[3]

Basic to the failure to make the adjustments necessary to the assimilation of increased power to produce goods is the "tendency toward saving a progressively increasing proportion of our income as our income itself gets larger."[4] This point (especially in a book devoted to Keynes) obviously deserves our closest attention, and it is worth while to quote the different formulations which Clark makes of what is nowadays called the "consumption function."

Note in particular the following: "A further fact is that at the peak, people with more income than usual are saving a larger percentage of it than usual, and spending a smaller percentage for consumers' goods. Thus demand for consumers' goods in general does not increase as fast as productive power . . . ."[5] Again in his *Strategic Factors in Business Cycles* he asserts that "there is the probability—which may be taken as a moral certainty—that as the national income increases in the upswing of the business cycle, consumers' expenditures increase less rapidly than the total income, and savings available for expenditures on producers' goods (or for advances on

---

[1] *Ibid.*, p. 114.

[2] Clark includes as the main items in the "mechanism by which private business takes care of the process" the following: (1) production in anticipation of demand, (2) an elastic credit system, (3) reduced prices of goods turned out at decreased unit costs, (4) wage cuts to help absorb displaced workers, (5) lower interest rates, (6) increased consumer spending due partly to investment outlays and partly to a wide distribution of business earnings.

[3] *Ibid.*, p. 113.

[4] *Ibid.*, p. 109.

[5] *Ibid.*, pp. 115–116.

the making of durable consumers' goods) increase more rapidly."[1]

If all savings, said Clark, were "automatically and promptly spent" on capital outlays of some sort, the "total demand for goods would be the same whether savings were large or small." But this does not "automatically happen."[2]

First we should seek, Clark argued, to stabilize the cycle, and we can then "face the further problem whether people spend too little for consumption, and save too much . . . and whether changes in the distribution of income can do something to improve the balance."[3]

Without waiting for the stabilization experiment, however, he offers the following reflections: "It is an unquestionable fact that the present system does not accomplish this task of adjustment successfully; and it is hardly open to question that the mere removal of booms and depressions would not furnish automatic solutions for all the problems of adjustment which would remain. Would the problem be solved if we could establish the completely fluid, freely-competitive system of individualistic theory?"[4] "To this question no scientifically proven answer can be given." But it is, he thought, "overwhelmingly probable" that such a system would still have booms and depressions. And the "processes of adjustment, even under the freest competition imaginable, would still take time and involve uncertainties, errors, and losses." Free com-

---

[1] *Strategic Factors in Business Cycles*, National Bureau of Economic Research, 1934, p. 78. The reader should note that these formulations of the functional relation of consumption to income are less cautious than that made by Keynes. Keynes limited himself to the proposition that the marginal propensity to consume is less than 1. In other words, as a community we save *some part* of an increment of income. Clark went further and argued that we save an increasing *proportion* of a rising income.

[2] *Ibid.*, p. 136.

[3] *Economic Reconstruction*, p. 120.

[4] *Ibid.*, p. 122.

petition "means competition which stands ready to go to unlimited cutthroat lengths." Greater flexibility in the system is
indeed desirable than that currently achieved, but that it
should "go the full lengths required to achieve the free-com-
petitive ideal is hardly thinkable; especially in the absence of
more definite assurance than can be given that the net result
would be to make us richer in the aggregate instead of
poorer."[1]

Among the special faults of the system he singled out "the
undue concentration of incomes and probably a resulting
tendency to over-saving, though the latter point needs fuller
investigation." If a more equal distribution "were achieved
mainly at the expense of reducing a volume of savings so
swollen that a considerable part of it goes to waste, the change
would be very nearly a clear gain."[2]

Clark's vigorous thinking illustrates, at its best, the pre-
Keynesian skepticism of neoclassical orthodoxy. But few took
any notice. What was required was nothing less than a *general
theory* sufficiently comprehensive to supplant the orthodox
theory of automatic adjustment. This truly herculean task
Keynes essayed in his *General Theory*.

THE BUSINESS CYCLE AND SAY'S LAW

As we have noted above, dissatisfaction with orthodox
theory sprang from the fact that the conclusions of theory often
failed to conform with the real world. Accordingly many economists, though unable to controvert orthodox logic, remained
unconvinced and deliberately turned their attention toward
more concrete problems. One such area which became increasingly popular in the period 1900 to 1936 was the business
cycle. But here it is necessary to make note of the fact that

[1] *Ibid.*, pp. 122–123.
[2] *Ibid.*, p. 125.

workers in this field included both adherents to and skeptics of the automatic-adjustment dogma of orthodox theory. It has often been said that the widespread theoretical pre-occupation with business-cycle problems in the period referred to is adequate proof that few, if any, economists any longer adhered to the doctrine of Say's law. I do not believe, however, that an examination of the literature will support this view.

Already J. S. Mill had an answer to the question whether Say's law was compatible with the *fact* of depression. Chapter XIV, Book III, of his *Principles* was devoted to an exposition supporting Say's doctrine. Yet Mill recognized the depressed state of the market which accompanies a commercial crisis. At such times "money demand," he said, is inadequate, and " . . . everyone dislikes to part with ready money, and many are anxious to procure it at any sacrifice." The depression may be called, he said, "a glut of commodities or a dearth of money." However, the more or less periodic occurrence of depressions was in no sense, he thought, a contradiction of Say's law. Depression is merely a "temporary derangement of markets." It is the consequence of an "excess of speculative purchases." Its immediate cause is a "contraction of credit," and the remedy is "the restoration of confidence."[1] Such disturbances in no way prove, he believed, that there are not powerful underlying forces tending to restore full employment equilibrium.

Mill regarded Say's law as extremely important. "The point is fundamental; any difference of opinion on it involves radically different conceptions of Political Economy, especially in its practical aspects."[2] If Say's law is not accepted, he said, then

[1] All these quotations are from p. 561 in Ashley's New Edition (November, 1909, and reprinted January, 1920) of J. S. Mill's *Principles of Political Economy*, first published in 1848.

[2] *Ibid.*, p. 562.

political economy must concern itself not merely with (1) the laws of production and (2) the laws of distribution but also with (3) the problem—"how a market can be created for produce," in other words, with the problem of adequate Aggregate Demand.

Marshall, in his *Principles* (1890), stood squarely with Mill. Indeed he not only quotes approvingly Mill's statement of Say's law but adds an analysis of business depressions identical to that offered by Mill. The chief cause of depression, he thought, is a want of confidence, largely the aftermath of reckless inflations of credit. When confidence is shaken, "though men have the power to purchase they may not choose to use it."[1]

F. M. Taylor, a rigorous thinker representing in the early twenties American orthodox economics at its best, expounded (in his *Principles*, 1921) Say's law and its relation to business depression on lines precisely similar to those of Mill and Marshall. He devoted a whole chapter to a strong endorsement of Say's law, and in particular the relation of business depression to that theory. Business depressions did not, in his opinion, disprove Say's law. Taylor viewed the law of markets as a valid long-run principle. But in the short run the exchange of products is broken, he explained, into two parts: products are first exchanged for money, and then money is exchanged for products. As Marshall put it, men have the power of purchase, but they may not use it, owing to temporary disturbances and maladjustments which destroy their confidence. These temporary disturbances were not regarded as invalidating in any way the deep-seated, fundamental forces (which

[1] Alfred Marshall, *Principles of Economics*, 7th ed., Macmillan & Co., Ltd. (London), p. 710. Note also the following: The only "effective remedy for unemployment is a continuous adjustment of means to ends, in such way that credit can be based on the solid foundation of fairly accurate forecasts" (p. 710).

Say's law sought to illuminate) tending automatically toward full employment.

Neoclassical writers on business cycles were usually concerned exclusively with *fluctuations*. The deeper question, whether or not the economy, despite these fluctuations, tended automatically toward full employment, was in the ordinary case not raised.[1] Typically, this automatic tendency was in fact assumed without question. A business-cycle theorist could quite consistently adhere to the basic principle of Say's law.

For the most part, economists avoided explicit reference to Say's law. But those, as in the case of Aftalion, who ventured to repudiate it were severely repulsed by the rigorous, orthodox logic which upheld the thesis of automatic adjustment. Others (like D. H. Robertson, to a degree the English counterpart of J. M. Clark) while making no general theoretical assault on the prevailing orthodoxy, remained vigorous skeptics and critics. Robertson did not pretend to know all the answers, but he raised awkward and uncomfortable questions. Far from being a complacent follower of the dogma of automatic adjustment, he probed deeply, relentlessly, and with tough-minded persistency, into the causes of the prevailing maladjustments.[2] In particular, attention should be called to his pioneer work on *hoarding* and its significance for the savings-investment problem.

Tugan-Baranowsky had already in his *Studien für Geschichte der Handelskrisen in England* (1901) propounded the disconcerting idea that a fundamental maladjustment may arise from a discrepancy between saving and investment. This was further elaborated by Wicksell in his *Lectures on Money* (1906) and

[1] As we have noted above, J. M. Clark (and doubtless others also) did raise this question.

[2] See his *A Study of Industrial Fluctuations*, P. S. King & Staples, Ltd. (London), 1915, *Banking Policy and the Price Level*, P. S. King & Staples, Ltd., 1926 and numerous articles in the *Economic Journal* and *Economica* and elsewhere during the decades of the twenties and thirties.

integrated with his earlier formulations (*Interest and Prices*, 1898) on the divergence between the natural rate and the money rate. Business-cycle theory was henceforth concerned, on the Continent at any rate, with something far more fundamental than mere credit and confidence disturbances. Henceforth, analysis relating to the dynamic role of investment, the relation of saving and investment, the innovational process, the time lags involved in the use of fixed capital, and the principle of derived demand (Tugan-Baranowsky, Wicksell, Spiethoff, Schumpeter, Aftalion) penetrated deeply not only into the special area of cycle theory[1] but also into general theoretical considerations with respect to the basic functioning of the economy as a whole. The deeper business-cycle theory probed into the problems referred to, the more urgent became the task of integrating monetary and cycle theory with the general theory of the price system.

PIGOU AND THE THEORY OF AUTOMATIC ADJUSTMENT

The Continental Investment analysis made scarcely any inroads on English thinking. This is particularly true of Pigou, and this fact has important consequences for his theory of employment, which was, and still remains, the most important challenge to the Keynesian thinking. In his *Industrial Fluctuations* (1927) Pigou remained skeptical of the role of autonomous investment, and there is no evidence that the Continental analysis of investment demand (Wicksell, Tugan-Baranowsky, Spiethoff) had ever become an integral part of his thinking. Discounting as he did the autonomous role of investment as a major determinant of fluctuations in Demand, he never became interested in the savings-investment analysis which held the center of the stage in Continental discussions. Industrial fluctuations, he believed, following Mill and Marshall, ema-

[1] See my *Business Cycles and National Income*, Part III.

nated mainly from disturbances relating to credit and confidence; yet his analysis was more rigorous than that of his predecessors especially by reason of his application of the principle of derived demand.

By ignoring the fundamental work of the Continental school on savings and investment, Pigou was able to view the business cycle as a temporary disturbance in an otherwise smoothly functioning system automatically tending toward full employment. There are indeed, he admitted, these recurring, short-run fluctuations in Demand. But they give rise, he thought, to fluctuations in employment only because wage rates are not sufficiently plastic. The more rigid wages are, the more employment will fluctuate. Chapter XIX (*Industrial Fluctuations*, Part I) on The Part Played by Rigidity in Wagerates is designed to explain that "if the wage-rate is perfectly plastic, the alteration in the quantity of labour at work will be nil."[1]

This thesis is reiterated in his *Theory of Unemployment* (1933), where he says: "With perfectly free competition . . . there will always be at work a strong tendency for wage-rates to be so related to demand that everybody is employed . . . . The implication is that such unemployment as exists at any time is due wholly to the fact that changes in demand conditions are continually taking place and that frictional resistances prevent the appropriate wage adjustments from being made instantaneously."[2] In his *Industrial Fluctuations* (Part II, Chap. IX) he advanced without reservation the view that a completely plastic wage policy would "abolish fluctuations of employment"[3] altogether. Thus Pigou stanchly supported the view

[1] *Industrial Fluctuations*, 1st ed., Macmillan & Co., Ltd. (London), 1927, p. 176.

[2] *Theory of Unemployment*, Macmillan & Co., Ltd. (London), 1933, p. 252.

[3] *Industrial Fluctuations*, p. 284. In fact, however, Pigou does not advocate complete wage flexibility, for social and practical reasons, but he does urge a more plastic wage policy.

that the system automatically tends toward full employment. Frictional maladjustments alone account for failure to utilize fully our productive power. Pigou entertained no doubt about the complete adequacy of neoclassical equilibrium theory.

As far as I am aware, Pigou never specifically mentioned Say's law. This, however, was due not to any doubts about its fundamental validity but rather, it may be inferred, to the fact that the older formulation of the law (J. B. Say, David Ricardo, James Mill, J. S. Mill, etc.) was cast in terms of a society that has largely passed away—a society in which most producers were typically self-employed individual proprietors, whether peasant farmers or master craftsmen. Either they raised farm produce or else they "manufactured"[1] products, and their income consisted of the sale of those products. To be "employed" meant simply to operate a farm or to set up a shop and to sell one's own output in the market. The proceeds were spent directly on tools, on farm and home buildings, and on consumers' goods. Saving *was* investment, not a distinct and separate process. The producer sold his *product*, not his *labor*. The greater the number of producers, the greater the size of the market. Products exchanged against products; supply created its own demand.

Now this statement does not fit the modern economy, in which saving and investment are distinct functions, and in which employment is found in a labor market and not by "setting up a shop." The older formulation of Say's law does not seem to apply to the present-day society. For Pigou the

---

Completely flexible wages (involving perhaps zero wages or even "negative wages") would, Pigou argued, "ensure full employment in all industries continuously, whatever changes demand might undergo" (p. 284). Zero or negative wages would of course involve the assumption that "wage-earners possess stores of goods." But who would buy the currently produced output? To this question Pigou gave no answer.

[1] "Manufacture" really meant, as the root words indicate, "made by hand."

problem related to the aggregate demand for labor. The Pigovian formulation of Say's law therefore ran in terms of the tendency of the economy, under free competition, to provide full employment in the labor market. And it was in these terms that he stated and restated the principle again and again in his *Industrial Fluctuations* (1927), *The Theory of Unemployment* (1933), the articles in the *Economic Journal* (September, 1937, December, 1943), *Employment and Equilibrium* (1941), and *Lapses from Full Employment* (1945).

In his *Theory of Unemployment* he argued that with free competition wage rates will tend to be so related to demand that everybody is employed.[1] One must concentrate attention upon two things: (1) the money-demand schedule for labor and (2) the money wage rate.

Pigou concluded that:[2]

> . . . the state of demand for labour, as distinguished from changes in that state, is irrelevant to employment, because wage-rates adjust themselves in such a manner that different states of demand, when once established, tend to be associated with similar average rates of unemployment. This implies that, from a long-period point of view, the real wage-rates for which people stipulate, so far from being independent of the demand function, are a function of that function in a very special way. . . . The implication is that such unemployment as exists at any time is due wholly to the fact that changes in demand conditions are continually taking place and that frictional resistances prevent the appropriate wage adjustments from being made instantaneously.

This statement is enormously important. It means that, whatever the state of Demand, there will always be, via wage adjustment, a tendency toward full employment. Thus any given state of Demand, once fully established, is as good as any other state. "If this broad conclusion is accepted it follows that

[1] Pigou, *Theory of Unemployment*, p. 252.
[2] *Ibid.*

long-run government policies, which . . . make the state of labour demand permanently better or worse than it would otherwise have been, are not, when once established, either causes of or remedies for unemployment."[1]

Now it was this theory of automatic adjustment, dominant in the current orthodoxy particularly as represented by Pigou, that Keynes attacked in his *General Theory*. The introduction (Book I) is devoted to a statement and critique of Say's law, and in particular to what I have called above the Pigovian formulation of Say's law.

Keynes was careful to state that he was making no attack on the neoclassical theory of value and distribution. This part of classical theory had been erected, he said, "with great care for logical consistency." Given the volume of employed resources, neoclassical theory was competent to explain how the product is divided among the factors. Moreover, useful and extensive study had been made of the volume of *available* resources (population, natural wealth, stock of capital goods). What was lacking, he believed, was a pure theory of the factors determining the actual *employment* of the available resources.

Pigou had in fact, in his *Theory of Employment*, distinguished between the *state* of Demand and *changes* in Demand. Pigou, as we have seen, believed that the state of Demand as such does not matter, as far as employment is concerned. But for Keynes this is not so. Thus the issue was joined. The controversy related to the postulates underlying the Pigovian formulation of Say's law, namely, the role of wage adjustment in the alleged automatic tendency toward full employment. "The matters at issue are," said Keynes, "of an importance which cannot be exaggerated" (*General Theory*, Preface, p. vi).[2]

[1] *Ibid.*, pp. 248–249.

[2] The page references, throughout this volume, which are inserted in the main body of the text are invariably to the *General Theory of Employment, Interest and Money*, Harcourt, Brace and Company, Inc., 1936, unless otherwise indicated.

Two powerful weapons, I repeat, were available with which to beat down any attack on the prevailing orthodoxy. They were (1) the rate of interest can be relied upon to adjust investment and savings so as to ensure (apart from temporary disturbances) full use of resources; (2) whatever the state of Demand, wage adjustment will always (apart from temporary disturbances) ensure full employment.

These then are the two doctrines upon which Keynes opened his assault—a probing maneuver—Chaps. 2 and 3. In the rest of the volume, fresh and more massive battalions were thrown into the conflict.

In Chap. 2 of the *General Theory*, Secs. I to V are devoted to the wages-demand adjustment thesis and Sec. VI to the doctrine that interest-rate adjustments automatically tend to solve the saving-investment problem. Both theses may be regarded as formulations of Say's law; and they stand or fall together. Keynes's substitution (see *General Theory*, Chap. 3) of the consumption function for Say's law was as essential for attacking the wages-demand analysis as for the assault on the classical saving-investment theory.

FLEXIBLE WAGES AND THE AUTOMATIC ADJUSTMENT PROCESS

In what I have said above, I have tried to answer a question students often ask: Why did Keynes begin with the postulates relating to wages? The answer is that in the classical (or neoclassical) analysis, wage-rate adjustment was an essential mechanism by which Say's law was supposed to function. Said Pigou, a year after the publication of the *General Theory:* "Until recently no economist doubted that an all-round reduction in the rate of money wages might be expected to increase, and an all-round enhancement to diminish, the volume of employment."[1]

[1] *Economic Journal*, September, 1937, p. 405.

Thus it was that Keynes plunged directly (Chap. 2) into a discussion of the classical postulates with respect to wage rates. He begins (p. 5) with two wages postulates. The first, which he accepted as valid, is the marginal-productivity theory of wages: "The wage is equal to the marginal product." Now the marginal product, if we assume organization, equipment, and technique as given in the short run (see p. 17), falls as employment increases. This follows from the law of diminishing marginal productivity. Thus real wage rates and employment are uniquely related; an increase of employment is associated, in equilibrium conditions, with lower real wage rates.[1]

On this point Keynes was emphatic. He accepted the marginal-productivity theory of wages. If industry is operating under decreasing returns (rising marginal cost), real wage rates must decline (in the short run) as employment is increased.[2]

These relationships *seem* to point to the conclusion that unemployment must be due to the refusal of workers "to accept a reward which corresponds to their marginal productivity" (p. 16). This Keynes denied. Instead he argued that unemployment was due to inadequate aggregate demand. Given the level of employment, the marginal product, and therefore the real wage, is indeed uniquely determined (assuming a given state of organization, equipment, and technique). Demand

[1] Keynes was a little too hasty in assuming that modern industry always operates under conditions of increasing marginal cost. (see my *Monetary Theory and Fiscal Policy*, McGraw-Hill Book Company, Inc., 1949, pp. 107–110). It should be noted here, however, that the critique there given in no way invalidates Keynes's fundamental thesis. That thesis is as follows: Classical doctrine is adequate to explain how any given product is divided between the factors, including the return to labor. It will tell you what the real wage rate will be, given the volume of employment; but it does not explain the volume of employment.

[2] I have critically examined Keynes's view with respect to the marginal-cost curve in Chap. 7 of my *Monetary Theory and Fiscal Policy*. See also Chap. 11 of this book.

determines employment, and employment determines the marginal product (*i.e.*, the real wage), not the other way round.

This brings us to the second classical postulate (p. 5). This postulate is made unnecessarily obscure by the fact that Keynes poses it in terms of the marginal disutility of labor in relation to the utility of the wage (*i.e.*, the *real* wage) associated with that given amount of employment. The postulate which Keynes attacked is in fact a bundle containing two very plain and simple propositions: (1) workers will refuse the proffer of employment if the *real* wage rate is cut below the current real wage; (2) a cut in *money* wage rates is an effective means to reduce real wage rates. These two propositions can be subsumed in the statement that the existing real wage is equal to the marginal disutility of employment. Keynes denied the validity of this postulate (pp. 5–13).

Keynes, it is important to remember, believed (as did also the classicals) that real wages and employment are inversely, but uniquely, related. If this be true, it then follows that unless the unemployed are prepared to accept jobs at current money wages (even though this may involve a cut in real wage rates) it would do no good to manipulate Demand along the lines of his own policy. If industry is operating under conditions of increasing marginal cost, and if wage earners insist that every rise in prices must be matched by a corresponding rise in money wages, then the only effect of increasing Demand would be price inflation with no increase in employment. If the utility of the current real wage is exactly equal to the marginal disutility of labor, it would not be possible to increase employment by raising Aggregate Demand. Thus it was essential for Keynes's theory to deny that workers will refuse employment at the current money wage whenever a small rise occurs in consumer prices. In Keynes's view, the existing real wage is not always equal to the marginal disutility of labor, and therefore labor may well be prepared to accept additional employment at current money wages even though this may mean lower real wages.

Keynes argued that workers are (within limits) quite prepared to accept the current *money* wage rate, if more employment is offered at that rate, even though, under increasing marginal-cost conditions, such increases in employment bring somewhat higher prices, and so lower real wage rates. This he believed to be an observable and indisputable fact, and he regarded it, moreover, as not illogical or unreasonable on the part of workers. Workers are, however, reluctant, he believed, to accept a cut in *money* wage rates (pp. 8–10).

The other element in the second classical postulate (namely, that acceptance by wage earners of money wage cuts would be an effective means of reducing real wage rates) he thought was theoretically more fundamental. This proposition he denied on the ground that the money income of wage earners *mainly* controls the total demand for consumers' goods. Thus if money wage rates (under the pressure of ruthless competition in the labor market) fall all round, the money-demand function for goods (and therefore the demand function for labor) will also fall.

The manipulation of wage rates is therefore, he thought, not an effective way to increase employment. Manipulation of Demand is a far more effective policy. With substantially stable money wage rates, employment could thereby be raised, and *as a result*, real wage rates (under conditions of increasing marginal cost) would fall to a level consistent with the increased volume of employment. Thus employment is not raised by cutting real wages. Rather it is the other way round: real wage rates fall *because* employment has been increased via an increase in demand. Real wage rates are not determined by the wage bargain; only the money wage is so determined. "There may exist no expedient by which labour as a whole can reduce its *real* wage to a given figure by making revised *money* bargains with the entrepreneurs" (p. 13). Other forces—those determining Aggregate Demand and employment—determine the level of real wages. Classical economics has quite rightly elucidated the forces which determine how the product is distributed among the factors when output and employment are given.

Consider the Pigovian equation[1] $N = \dfrac{qY}{W}$, in which N is employment, q is that fraction of national income earned as wages and salaries, Y is the national income (which in equilibrium is equal to aggregate demand for output), and W is the money wage rate. Now the essence of this part of the Keynesian analysis (if one applies it to the Pigovian equation) is that, if W is cut, Y will fall more or less proportionately, leaving little effect on N unless q changes (for example, under the impact of the substitution of labor for other factors in view of the fall in money wages).

It is clear that Keynes reached no rigorous conclusion, and he later reassessed the whole complicated problem in Chap. 19. The analysis in Chap. 2, however, does point up the fact that the effect of a cut in wages is *mainly* to cut Aggregate Demand, leaving employment at best relatively unaffected. This statement, as we shall see, needs elaboration and qualification.

A diagrammatic explanation may perhaps clarify the analysis. In Fig. 1, N (*i.e.*, employment) is measured on the horizontal axis; W (*i.e.*, money wage rates) on the vertical axis. ϕ_L is the demand function for labor; it is the curve showing the functional relation of N to W.

Now ϕ_L, the money-demand function for labor, will obviously shift up or down as Aggregate Demand Y rises or falls. Thus *if* a cut in W causes Y to fall proportionally, N will re-

[1] A. C. Pigou, *Agenda*, August, 1944.

main constant. In terms of Fig. 1, a cut in wages from W_1 to W_2 will cause a corresponding drop in ϕ_L from curve Y_1 to Y_2. Accordingly N is left unchanged at N_a. But this assumes that a change in W causes a proportionate change in Y, while no

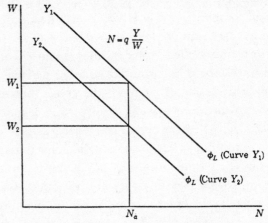

FIG. 1. Wage rates and employment.

change occurs in q. Just what will in fact happen, under different conditions, is a very complicated problem, and we shall have much more to say about it in Chap. 10.

THE PRINCIPLE OF EFFECTIVE DEMAND

Chapter 3 of the *General Theory* is a highly important part of Keynes's epoch-making book. This chapter is of special significance because here, after repeated failures, an impressive attack was at long last made upon Say's law.

Yet this chapter could not have been written had there not evolved a new way of looking at the factors behind the Aggregate Demand for output. This new way of thinking about the problem stems from Wicksell (1898), Tugan-Baranowsky (1901), and Spiethoff (1902).[1]

[1] See my *Business Cycles and National Income, op. cit.* Part III.

Basically there are two approaches to the problem of Aggregate Demand: the MV approach and the $I + C$ approach.[1] The fundamental difference between them can very briefly be put as follows: The MV approach conceives of Demand as a global quantity, and not as an aggregate of independently determined component parts. Given a certain volume of monetary demand MV, the *kinds* of things that will be purchased depend simply upon the relative utilities and prices of different goods. If one thing is not wanted, another *will* be. Under a flexible price and wage system, all the goods that the system can produce will automatically tend to find a market. And the *magnitude* of MV, be it noted, is not regarded as important from the standpoint of ensuring an adequate market or full use of resources; the magnitude of MV is important only as a determinant of the level of prices and of money wage rates. Those who are accustomed to look at the matter through the MV glasses find it very difficult to conceive of any problem of inadequate Aggregate Demand.

The $I + C$ approach stresses the fact that a society which uses large quantities of fixed capital—in modern societies the capital *stock* may be around three times an annual output— operates on fundamentally different principles from one which applies labor directly (though aided by simple hand tools) to the production of consumers' goods. In a capitalistic society, Demand is directed toward two quite distinct kinds of products, (1) consumers' goods and (2) investment goods. The elements determining the demand for investment goods are very different from those determining the demand for consumers' goods. Demand for consumers' goods depends mainly upon the purchasing power (*i.e.*, the income) of consumers; demand

---

[1] By MV is meant the Quantity Theory approach, which emphasizes the role of the quantity, M, and the velocity, V, of money. By $I + C$ is meant the income-expenditure approach, which emphasizes the role of investment outlays, I, and consumption outlays, C.

for investment goods depends upon expectations of profitability, and this demand *may* be low even though ample funds are available for their purchase. On the other hand, if expectations are favorable for investment, though funds are currently lacking, means of purchase can readily be made available in a society with an elastic money and credit system. Wicksell put it as follows: "Abundance or scarcity of money, and in particular the quantity of cash held by the banks, is now imbued with a merely secondary importance."[1]

The division of Aggregate Demand into investment outlays and consumption outlays for purposes of income analysis represented a revolution in thinking. The investment-demand analysis of Wicksell was incorporated by Keynes into his system, but he added one significant element, namely, the role of the liquidity preference function in the determination of the rate of interest.

Keynes's most notable contribution, however, was his consumption function. The psychological propensities of consumers plus the institutional behavior patterns of the community (notably those of business firms) are such, he argued, that (1) some part of income (except at very low levels) is saved and (2) of any net *addition* to real income, some of the increment is saved. Accordingly, the behavior patterns of the community are such that a gap exists (which gap widens *absolutely* as real income increases) between the amount the community wishes to consume and the output the community is capable of producing. Thus the degree to which the system can find a market for its potential output depends, given the functional relation of consumption to income, upon the volume of investment as determined by those special factors which control investment expenditures.

This analysis represents a fundamental attack on Say's law.

[1] Knut Wicksell, *Interest and Prices*, The Macmillan Company, 1936, p. 167.

Aftalion, indeed, had said that consumption (owing to the law of diminishing marginal utilities) increases *absolutely* less than output; and J. M. Clark, basing his conclusion on general knowledge and observation, had made an explicit and clear statement of this relation. But both had failed to clinch their points. Keynes, however, was able to make a deeper impression largely because he integrated this new tool of analysis— the consumption function—with other relevant functions to formulate a general theory of income and employment.

Keynes's analysis reveals that the essential defect in Say's law is that it confuses an *indubitable* proposition, namely, that the income derived by all the productive factors springs from the sale of the output (p. 20), with the *invalid* proposition that therefore all *costs* of output will necessarily be covered by the sales proceeds. The second proposition is mistakenly inferred from the first. Current income is indeed derived from current sale proceeds. And current production is undertaken in *expectation* of sale proceeds adequate to cover all costs (including normal profits). But sale proceeds are determined by the demand for consumers' goods plus the demand for investment goods. Aggregate Demand $I + C$ may not equal the Aggregate Supply price (Aggregate Cost of output). And the reason is (1) that, while consumer demand is indeed primarily a function of current income it does not rise as much as income and (2) the demand for investment goods is largely determined by factors (technological developments, etc.) unrelated to current income. Entrepreneurs are likely to base their sales expectations on current demand. They therefore tend to anticipate sale proceeds which will equal the Aggregate Cost of output. But this expectation may prove false in view of the exogenous factors which *autonomously* determine the demand for investment goods.[1]

[1] It may perhaps be said that the conventional distinction between autonomous and induced investment is an artificial dichotomy—that in

The increased capital stock associated with the increased requirements of a progressing society is determined by (1) the development of technique, which affects the technical coefficients[1] of the factors of production and the per worker productivity, and (2) the growth of the labor force. Given the consumption function, the demand for investment goods, so determined, may not provide full employment.

The determinants of consumption and the determinants of investment are not interconnected in a manner which ensures an adequate Aggregate Demand so that sale proceeds will necessarily tend to equal the Aggregate Cost of a growing full-employment output.

The relevant schedules are (1) the schedule relating Aggregate Supply price to output and (2) the schedule relating sale proceeds to output. The former may be called the Aggregate Supply schedule and the latter the Aggregate Demand schedule. The intersection of these two schedules will determine the particular volume of output at which sale proceeds equal Aggregate Cost. But this may not be a full-employment output.

At every point in the Aggregate Demand schedule, D (*i.e.*, total Demand) consists of two elements D_1, Demand for consumers' goods, and D_2, Demand for investment goods. For the

---

fact *all* investment is in a fundamental sense related to expectations with respect to the growth of real income. The purpose of all production is indeed consumption. Investment has no purpose except to provide consumers' goods. *All* investment is thus regarded as a function of a growing real income. From this standpoint the division of Aggregate Demand into $I + C$ is thought to be less significant since I is closely linked to C. But even so, there is no reason to suppose that the investment-demand function and the consumption-demand function must necessarily be such that the sum of the marginal propensities to purchase investment goods and consumption goods would be unity. Indeed the Keynesian analysis leads to a quite different conclusion.

[1] "Technical coefficients" refers to the quantities of the different factors required, under given technical conditions of production, to produce a given quantity of a certain good or commodity.

D_1 element, Keynes advanced, as we have seen, the hypothesis that consumption (in real terms) is a function of real income. And since real income (or output) will vary in the short run (given the state of organization, equipment, and technique) with the volume of employment, we may also say that consumption is a function of employment. This function (schedule or curve) relating consumption outlays to employment he calls $\chi(N)$. The D_2 part of Aggregate Demand will be considered presently.

The schedule of sale proceeds required to cover the cost (*i.e.*, the payments to all factors including normal profits) of producing the output associated with the employment of varying quantities of labor, Keynes called Z. Table 1 is an illustrative table showing the numerical values of Z for different quantities of O (output) and N (employment). Z is the Aggregate Supply price of output from employing N workers. Thus $Z = \phi N$.

Table 1

Z Aggregate supply price of output in constant-value dollars, billions	O Output base year = 100	N Number of workers employed, millions
300	100	60
270	90	54
240	80	50
200	67	40

Now we have seen that consumption is a function of real income, or output, O, and therefore also a function of N, the employment associated with a given output. Thus $D_1 = \chi(N)$. In order to call forth a certain output O and the employment N associated therewith, the Aggregate Demand D (that is, $D_1 + D_2$, in which D_1 stands for consumption and D_2 for investment outlays) would have to be sufficient so that the sale proceeds will cover the cost of output. Thus at each level of O

(and N), $D_1 + D_2$ must be equal to Z. Therefore, given the two functions $Z = \phi(N)$ and $D_1 = \chi(N)$, it follows that the varying quantities of D_2 required to call forth each level of output O and employment N is the difference between Z and D_1 at each point in the schedule. Thus $D_2 = \phi(N) - \chi(N)$. In Fig. 2 the quantity of investment D_2 required for each level of output and employment is the difference between curve ϕ and curve χ.

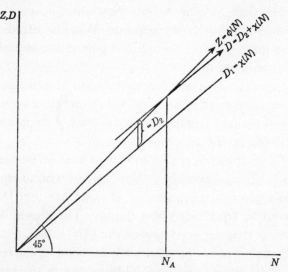

Fig. 2. Aggregate Demand and Aggregate Supply. *Note:* Realized employment (N_A) is determined by the intersection of the Aggregate Demand function, $D_2 + x(N)$, and the Aggregate Supply function, $\phi(N)$.

Thus for each *realized* level of output and employment, $D_1 + D_2 = D = Z$. Now D_2, is largely a function of exogenous factors (technology and population) and is not fixed by O and N; and since D_2 is not determined by N, therefore D is not determined by N. It is true that the virtual points in the schedule Z will not be realized (*i.e.*, become "observable" points) unless $D = Z$. Given the $\phi(N)$ and the $\chi(N)$ functions, we know what volume of D_2 is necessary to call forth a given quantity of output and employment.

Keynes is wrong (p. 29) when he makes $D = \phi(N)$. Points in D which have become observable and the points in Z which have become observable are indeed always equal, but it is an error to say that D is a function of N. Z (not D) is a function of N, that is, $Z = \phi(N)$; and D_1 is a function of N, that is, $D_1 = \chi(N)$. Now $D_2 = \phi(N) - \chi(N)$. Indeed to make $D = \phi(N)$, when $Z = \phi(N)$ would be the same as saying that the Aggregate Demand function is identical to the Aggregate Supply function, in other words, Say's law. Keynes's argument in fact is precisely the opposite. What he means to say should be quite evident, though this part of the exposition is certainly confusing.

The Aggregate Demand function should indeed have been written as follows: $D = D_2 + \chi(N)$. As we have seen, D_2 is largely autonomously determined, though it is in part a function of *changes* in N.[1]

There is no inherent reason to believe that investment outlays plus consumption outlays would always tend to equal the cost of any given output; there is no assurance that Demand would tend to equal *any* given Supply. The reason for this conclusion is that the gap between the $\chi(N)$ schedule and the $\phi(N)$ schedule will not automatically be filled by the requisite volume of investment outlays. The maximum maintainable volume of investment is determined by the laws of growth of the economy, *i.e.*, by technologically determined capital requirements of a progressive society which enjoys increasing per capita productivity and a growing labor force. D_2, the demand for investment goods, is determined, basically, by changes in technology and in population growth, and in the short run by all sorts of expectations. Investment demand, so

---

[1] It is probable that new techniques would be exploited more fully at high- (in contrast with low-) income levels. In this sense, autonomous investment may perhaps be regarded as a function of the level of income. See article by Harrod in *Economic Journal*, June, 1951.

determined, will not necessarily fill the gap between $\phi(N)$ and $\chi(N)$. But according to classical theory "there is some force in operation which, when employment increases, always causes D_2 to increase sufficiently to fill the widening gap between Z and D_1" (p. 30).

It could indeed be argued that $\chi(N)$ would tend over time to shift to a level such that $D_2 + \chi(N)$ would equal Z at full-employment. The study of such long-run adjustment processes is in its infancy, and we know as yet very little about it. Long-run adjustments are, we know, partly volitional (deliberate social reform designed to cure deep-seated maladjustments) and partly automatic. A historical study of long-run automatic adjustments could never be conclusive since such adjustments are always commingled with conscious adjustment processes. Thus, prior to and after the Second World War, it is evident that the growth of the "welfare state" (consciously and deliberately established) in all advanced democracies was bringing about a redistribution of income which tended to raise the consumption function $\chi(N)$. Whether, in addition to this movement, an *automatic* long-run adjustment was also being made so that $D_2 + \chi(N)$ would tend to equal Z at full employment is a matter which cannot be definitely established one way or the other. At all events, it may well be that, in this area of long-run adjustments, it may be possible, in a measure, to find a reconciliation between Keynesian and neoclassical economics. Keynes was dealing with behavior patterns of the community (social institutions and psychological laws) which are fairly stable in terms of the relatively short run, *i.e.*, one, two, or three decades. He did not claim that these behavior patterns are fixed for all time and, especially, that they could not be *consciously* changed. The area of long-run adjustment processes (including both the conscious and the purely automatic) deserves much more study than it has so far received from economists.

The gist of the matter, then, is this: Say's law is not valid because consumption in real terms rises absolutely less than output, or real income, Y (*i.e.*, the marginal propensity to consume[1] $\dfrac{\Delta C}{\Delta Y}$ is less than unity) and this widening gap may or may not be filled by investment depending upon the prevailing

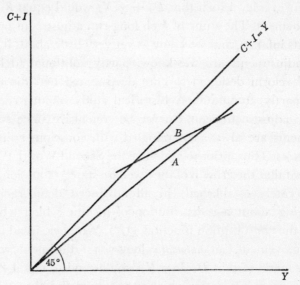

FIG. 3. Two consumption functions, A and B.

strength of the factors (technology and population growth) which determine the volume of investment outlays.

The slope of the consumption function (*i.e.*, the marginal propensity to consume being in greater or smaller degree less than unity) is indeed a necessary pillar for the overthrow of Say's law. But it is not sufficient. In addition, it must also be shown that there is no reason to suppose that the price system will operate in a manner so that investment outlays will

[1] Here we jump ahead a little and assume that since employment N and output, or real income Y, are likely to fluctuate together in the short run, the functional relation $D_1 = \chi(N)$ can equally well be stated as $C = C(Y)$.

automatically tend to fill the ever-widening gap, in absolute terms, between consumption and output.

In this connection it is necessary to stress the point that Keynes did not say that consumption rises *proportionally* less than output. The Keynesian condition would be satisfied by a consumption function starting at point of origin (at O as in curve A in Fig. 3). If the function is linear, this would mean that the marginal propensity to consume is equal to the average propensity to consume at all income levels but that the curve lies somewhat below the 45° angle curve. Keynes, however, believed, (and empirical data tend to support this view, that the slope of the function is in fact flatter, as in curve B (Fig. 3), at least over a wide range of the cycle. In this case the marginal propensity to consume will vary from the average propensity to consume.

In Chap. 3 we shall have something to say about the slope of the "secular" consumption function and its relation to the "cyclical" consumption function.[1]

---

[1] Keynes slipped into another error—a minor point on p. 31. It relates to the propensity to consume in a wealthy community. He confuses the *level* of the consumption function with the *slope* of the function. Very poor countries are able to save (and invest) only a very small per cent of even a full-employment income; the average propensity to save is very low. Wealthy (industrially developed) countries are able to save and invest a large per cent of a full-employment income; the average propensity to save is relatively high. But it does not necessarily follow that the *marginal* propensity to consume is lower in the wealthy than in the poor countries unless, indeed, the functions are linear and start at point of origin. That may or may not be the case. Keynes was not sufficiently careful here (as elsewhere) to distinguish between the average and the marginal propensity to consume.

Book Two
Definitions and Ideas

CHAPTER 2

General Concepts

1. THE CHOICE OF UNITS (GENERAL THEORY, CHAPTER 4)

Book II of the *General Theory* is a detour. The argument which was commenced in Book I is interrupted and resumed in Book III. The intervening chapters, 4 to 7, are devoted to preliminary definitions and concepts which logically might better have been treated at the outset of the volume. But Keynes wanted the reader to get a taste of what was coming first. Accordingly, he postponed to Book II the dry and rather uninteresting consideration of the concepts and terms employed in the argument which followed. Chapter 5, however, dealing with *expectations and dynamics*, should certainly be singled out as of quite exceptional interest and importance.

He begins with a chapter on The Choice of Units. In all modern economics, in fact, the *monetary* unit is employed as the standard of measurement in the market place. But for purposes of *economic analysis* the monetary unit will not do. And the reason (well-recognized by the early founders of the science) is that economic analysis proceeds by setting up functional relations between variables. If now the empirical data, given in monetary values, apply to a period in which the value of money or, inversely, the price level changed substantially, spurious relations between the variables in question will appear. This is true because, if all prices double (value of money is cut in two), then one of the two things will happen: (1) in the transition a lagging adjustment between variables will show up which distorts the "true" normal relationship of the variables, as, for example, a lag of wages behind the movement of consumer's prices; (2) the variables (lags assumed overcome) will all have changed *in the same proportion*. For

39

example, if income in money terms has doubled, consumption (in money terms) would also be doubled, the lags having been worked through. Consumption would therefore have increased proportionally with income. Both increases are, however, due solely to a change in the unit of measurement. Neither income nor consumption, in real terms, has changed. But when we consider *analytically* the relation of consumption to income, we are interested to know how consumption changes when income *in real terms* rises. If we can disregard short-run lags, purely nominal increases of income cannot be expected to produce changes in the relation of consumption to income; a change in real income *might*, however, be expected to alter the relation of consumption to income.

Thus functional relationships between economic variables can have little meaning or significance unless the variables are measured in real terms. Monetary units of measurement will not do. The data are, however, necessarily cast in money terms. It therefore becomes necessary to reduce the monetary magnitudes to real terms; in other words, to correct for nominal changes, *i.e.*, reduce monetary magnitudes to *real* magnitudes.

Economic literature discloses two leading points of view with respect to the problem of how best to reduce numerical values expressed in monetary (*i.e.*, nominal) units to real values. One school has suggested that the nominal, or monetary, values be corrected for changes in the purchasing power of money with respect to goods. Thus the *nominal* data (expressed in the monetary units current in the period covered by the data) are reduced to *real* terms by correcting for changes in the price level of goods. The dollars used are then no longer nominal dollars; they are "constant-value" dollars.

The second school has suggested the view that *real* values can best be obtained by correcting the nominal figures for changes in money wage rates. This being done, the data would then be expressed in "constant-wage" dollars.

The essential difference between these two methods can be illustrated from Figs. 4 and 5.

In Fig. 4 two charts are presented, *A* and *B*. Chart *A* gives the growth in national income *Y*, measured in current dollars, together with a curve *P*, showing price movements. Chart *B* shows the growth in income measured in constant-value dollars (*i.e.*, the nominal-value dollar magnitudes are corrected by using a properly weighted index of prices as a deflator). The resulting curve gives the movement of real income, or

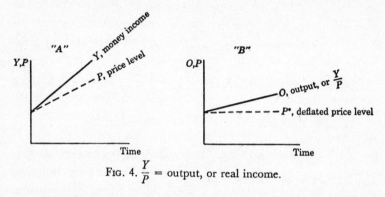

FIG. 4. $\frac{Y}{P}$ = output, or real income.

output. Curve *O*, in other words, shows what the national income would have been had prices remained constant. If *P* and *Y* are known, *O* can be derived from equation $PO = Y$; or

$$O = \frac{Y}{P}.$$

Figure 5 similarly shows two charts, *A* and *B*. Chart *A* gives again the national income *Y* in current dollars and also the movement of money wage rates *W*. Chart *B* gives the national income measured in constant wage rates (*i.e.*, the nominal-value dollar magnitudes are corrected by using an index of money wage rates as a deflator). Curve *B* shows, in other words, what the change in the money value of the national income would have been had money wage rates remained constant. With money wage rates constant, the national income expressed in terms of dollars would have remained constant unless a change had occurred (1) in employment N or (2) in the *proportion* of income paid out in wages and salaries, q, or in both. Assuming no change in the per cent of total income received in wages and salaries (q is usually more or less around 65 per cent), and assuming wage rates constant, then changes in the total national income would reflect changes in

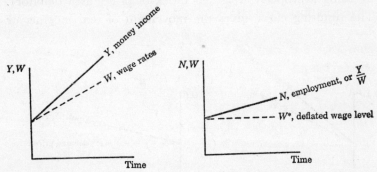

FIG. 5. $\dfrac{Y}{W}$ = employment. *Note:* Wage income is here assumed to be a constant fraction of total money income.

employment as shown in curve N. In short if Y, q, and W are known, then N can be derived from the equation $WN = qY$; or $N = q\,\dfrac{Y}{W}$.

Thus, correcting for *price* changes, the deflated national-income figures would give changes in output (*i.e.*, real income). But correcting for *wage-rate* changes, the deflated national-income figures would give changes in employment.

Keynes adopted (for convenience of exposition) a short-run analysis in which organisation, equipment, and technique are assumed as given. On this basis employment and output could be expected to fluctuate closely together, and similarly wage rates and prices would likely move closely in unison. Thus for Keynes it really made no great difference whether he corrected the nominal monetary magnitudes by a price index or by a wage-rate index. But if a longer run view is taken, a considerable divergence could be expected in the movements of output and employment. By reason of the tendency for man-hour productivity to increase over time, output would outrun employment, and prices would fall relative to the movement of wage rates. Thus from the longer run standpoint, the choice of the deflator is highly important. If the nominal data are corrected for price changes, the deflated figures will show changes in output; if such data are corrected for wage-rate changes, the deflated figures will disclose changes in employment.

Both methods are acceptable as procedures whereby data expressed in *nominal* monetary magnitudes can be reduced to real terms. Keynes, however, chose to use the money-wage-rate[1] index as his deflator.

He did this because he believed that the units employed in the measurement of employment and wages are less equivocal than those designed to measure output and prices. Employment, he suggested, can be measured in terms of labor units. A "labor unit" may be taken to mean one hour of work by ordinary, or common, labor. An hour's skilled work could, he thought, be weighted in proportion to its remuneration in relation to that of common labor. Thus if skilled labor is paid twice as much as common labor per hour, then one hour of skilled work may be regarded as equal quantitatively to two labor units. Now the wage unit is the *money wage paid for one labor unit*.

In fact, Keynes's labor-unit method of measuring the volume of employment for a country with a population possessing a vast variety of skills and undergoing major changes with respect to the structure and composition of jobs and occu-

[1] Keynes's "wage unit" is the money wage rate paid for one hour of common labor.

pations, together with structural changes in wage differentials, is far from being unequivocal. It is no more satisfactory than the methods commonly employed by economists to construct index numbers designed to measure movements of prices, output, or the stock of capital. Keynes regarded these latter methods as not sufficiently precise for the purposes of causal analysis (pp. 37–39). But his arguments are far from being convincing. With respect to the problem of index numbers there is a large, controversial, and highly technical literature. This literature and the methods which have been devised disclose the vast complexity of the subject matter of economics. Unequivocal statistical results cannot, in the nature of the case, be reached. The extreme purist had best not pursue the field of economics. But it is the general consensus that the methods devised and the results reached are tolerably satisfactory for both analytical and practical purposes. "Output," "capital stock," and the "general price level" are usable concepts, and their magnitudes are, within reason, measurable.

Keynes's analysis could have proceeded quite as well had he adopted the price index as his deflator instead of his wage unit. For his purposes either method would do. Whether one uses constant-value dollars or constant-wage-unit dollars, either method can be regarded as a reasonably satisfactory means of reducing nominal (*i.e.*, monetary) magnitudes to real terms. Fundamentally the matter is of no great consequence. On balance Keynes's readers would probably have preferred constant-value dollars to constant-wage-unit dollars.

2. EXPECTATIONS AND DYNAMICS (GENERAL THEORY, CHAPTER 5)

Keynes felt that he could not effectively proceed with his argument without introducing, in a preliminary way, a discussion of expectations. He returns to this theme again and again.

J. R. Hicks, in his first review article on the *General Theory* (*Economic Journal*, June, 1936), singles out this feature for special mention. The "use of the method of expectations," said Hicks, "is perhaps the most revolutionary thing about this book."[1] Keynes believed that the current economic theory was frequently unrealistic because it assumed too often a "static state where there is no changing future to influence the present."[2]

The *General Theory* is, however, cast mainly in terms of equilibrium analysis. Keynes's method, in much of the book, can indeed be described as comparative statics. But in his hands comparative statics becomes a useful device for thinking about practical problems in a manner which is essentially dynamic. Hicks was the first to see this quite clearly. "It is a theory of shifting equilibrium *vis-a-vis* the static or stationary theories of general equilibrium such as those of Ricardo, Böhm-Bawerk, or Pareto."[3]

In static analysis, certain parameters such as tastes, income, etc., being assumed as given, a functional relation is posited between two variables, say price and quantity demanded. At a higher price less will be demanded. But this is purely static analysis. If a change in anticipations is introduced so that prices are expected to rise further, Demand will probably increase—*more* will be purchased in anticipation of further price increases. This represents a dynamic situation. If a given *higher* price is regarded as permanent, the static Demand schedule will again control the quantity taken. But if it is expected that prices will continue to rise, a higher price will call forth an increase in Demand; *i.e.*, under the impact of the element of anticipations the static Demand schedules will shift up or to the

[1] J. R. Hicks, "Mr. Keynes' Theory of Employment," *Economic Journal*, June, 1936, p. 240.

[2] Keynes, *General Theory*, p. 145.

[3] Hicks, *op. cit.*, p. 238.

right. The *change* from one equilibrium position to another is the subject matter of comparative statics. Comparative statics is a study of "the way in which our equilibrium quantities will change as a result of changes in the parameters taken as independent data."[1]

Comparative statics should assist us to discern the direction and magnitude of changes in the variables when certain data change so as to cause a movement to a new equilibrium condition. Pareto, says Samuelson, "laid the basis for a theory of *comparative statics* by showing how a change in a datum would displace the position of equilibrium."[2]

In comparative-statics analysis, we investigate "the response of a system to changes in given parameters."[3] In *period analysis* and in *rates-of-change analysis* we investigate the behavior of the system which results from the passage of time. Comparative statics leaps over the time involved in the transition to the successive positions of equilibrium. But in period analysis we have an economy *in motion*, an economy *undergoing change*. Comparative statics "involves the special case where a 'permanent' change is made, and only the effects upon final levels of stationary equilibrium are in question."[4] Dynamic analysis proper gives us a "description of the actual path followed by a system in going from one 'comparative static level' to another."[5]

Hicks pointed out that the subject matter for Keynes's study and analysis was not the "norm of the static state," but rather the changing, progressing, fluctuating economy." This has "to be studied on its own, and cannot usefully be referred to the norm of the static state." Accordingly, while static

[1] Samuelson, *Foundations of Economic Analysis*, Harvard University Press, 1947, p. 257.
[2] *Ibid.*, p. 351.
[3] *Ibid.*
[4] *Ibid.*, p. 352.
[5] *Ibid.*

theory has ordinarily assumed that tastes and resources are given, Keynes introduced into his comparative statics a new and vitally significant element, namely, "people's anticipations of the future."[1] "Once the missing element—anticipations—is added, equilibrium analysis can be used, not only in the remote stationary conditions to which many economists have found themselves driven back, but even in the real world, even in the real world in 'disequilibrium.' "[2]

Thus while Keynes's method is formally that of comparative statics, it is nonetheless a highly useful method of studying an economy undergoing change. "The equations of comparative statics are then a special case of the general dynamic analysis."[3]

In Keynes's method the lagging adjustment that the economic system makes in response to the introduction of a disturbance is indeed often skipped over, and attention is directed to the equilibrium (or normal) magnitudes and relationships of the relevant variables. Now it is the system's power of adjustment or adaptation (not indeed the lagged response, but the *normal* or *equilibrium* response) that primarily interests Keynes. "The point of the method," said Hicks, "is that it reintroduces determinateness into a process of change."[4] The method is, he concludes, "an admirable one for analysing the impact effect of disturbing causes."[5]

That the *General Theory* is fundamentally a study of the "economy in motion" is evident throughout the book, and it is generally admitted that its publication, and the discussions to which it gave rise, gave a powerful stimulus to the study of dynamics. It has helped to make us think of economics in dynamic rather than in static terms. The "usefulness of the

[1] Hicks, *op. cit.*, p. 240.
[2] *Ibid.*
[3] Samuelson, *op. cit.*, p. 262.
[4] Hicks, *op. cit.*, p. 241.
[5] *Ibid.*

Keynesian equilibrium system lies in the light it throws upon the way our unknowns will change as a result of changes in data."[1]

Moreover, on occasion Keynes went beyond the method of comparative statics and employed the method of dynamic economics. Here and there the argument in fact proceeds in terms of period analysis, as when he discusses the expenditure lag in the multiplier process (pp. 122–124). At other times it proceeds in terms of time rates of change as in the case of perfect anticipation of consumers and of the suppliers of consumers' goods to continuous changes in investment outlays (pp. 124–125). Here consumption moves, without time lag, in a continuous equilibrium relation to income (moving equilibrium; continuous functions).

We now turn to a brief consideration of various concepts of dynamic analysis.

Ragnar Frisch conceived dynamic theory to be one in which:[2]

> . . . we consider not only a set of magnitudes in a given point of time and study the inter-relations between them, but we consider the magnitudes of certain variables in different points of time, and we introduce certain equations which embrace at the same time several of those magnitudes belonging to different instants. This is the essential characteristic of a dynamic theory. Only by a theory of this type can we explain how one situation grows out of the foregoing.

An illustration is the Robertsonian period analysis involving the expenditure lag. The consumption of today, C_1, is a function of yesterday's income Y_0, while the income of today is generated out of the consumption and investment expenditures

[1] Samuelson, *op. cit.*, p. 277.

[2] Ragnar Frisch, Propagation Problems and Impulse Problems in Dynamic Economics, *Economic Essays in Honor of Gustav Cassel*, George Allen & Unwin, Ltd. (London), 1933, pp. 171–172.

of today. Thus let t represent a certain period; then $t - 1$ is the preceding period. We then get the following difference (lag) equations:

$$Y_t = C_t + I_t$$
$$C_t = C(Y_{t-1})$$
$$Y_t = C(Y_{t-1}) + I_t$$

Applying the Robertsonian period analysis we see, in view of the expenditure lag as expressed in the equation $C_t = C(Y_{t-1})$, how the multiplier process works itself out over time. Period analysis represents a dynamic theory in the respect that it discloses the *process* of change over time.

Following Frisch, Hicks defined economic dynamics as "those parts where every quantity must be dated."[1]

Harrod, however, defines dynamics as the study of an "economy in which the rates of output are changing."[2] Dynamics, says Harrod, has to do with "continuing changes generated by the special nature of a growing economy."[3] Classical economics he thought contained both static and dynamic elements in roughly equal proportions. Net realized saving, for example, represents growth of capital, and this, says Harrod, was rightly regarded by Ricardo as a dynamic concept.[4] Dynamic economics must concern itself with "the necessary relations between the rates of growth of the different elements in a growing economy."[5]

Lagged variables may produce mere oscillation, and such a process of change over time fully satisfies Frisch's definition of dynamics. In my own view, however, mere oscillation represents a relatively unimportant part of economic dynamics.

---

[1] J. R. Hicks, *Value and Capital*, Oxford University Press, 1939, p. 115.
[2] R. G. Harrod, *Towards a Dynamic Economics*, Macmillan & Co., Ltd. (London), 1948, p. 4.
[3] *Ibid.*, p. 11.
[4] *Ibid.*, pp. 15–16.
[5] *Ibid.*, p. 19.

Growth, not oscillation, is the primary subject matter for study in economic dynamics. Growth involves changes in technique and increases in population. Indeed that part of cycle literature (and cycle theories are a highly significant branch of dynamic economics) which is concerned merely with oscillation is rather sterile. Among the great contributions to business-cycle theory are those (Tugan-Baranowsky, Spiethoff, Schumpeter, Cassel) which are primarily concerned with growth.

From the period-analysis point of view, dynamics deals with time lags, lagged adjustments (difference or lag equations) in a process of change. This type of theory is dynamic in that some variables are thought to depend on the lagged values of other variables.[1] From Harrod's point of view, however, dynamics deals with *rates of change* (differential equations), and the theory is dynamic in the respect that the rates of change of certain variables are thought to depend on the rates of change of other variables. In the latter case there are no time lags. Instead there is a moving equilibrium in which the variables are always in a normal or equilibrium relation to one another. The *actual* magnitudes of the variables are always equal to the *desired* magnitudes. The Keynesian "moving-equilibrium multiplier" represents this case. The variables are continuously at a normal or equilibrium relation to each other (continuous functions).

Thus in certain sections of the *General Theory* the analysis is cast in terms of time rates of change in a moving equilibrium. This represents perfect foresight and continuous adjustment to change, so that the *actual* magnitudes of the different variables always correspond to the *desired* magnitudes. This is a time rate-of-change analysis. We are here dealing with *continuous* functions, and the system is in a state of moving equilibrium.

[1] See R. M. Goodwin in Alvin H. Hansen, *Business Cycles and National Income*, W. W. Norton & Company, 1951, p. 420.

The *General Theory* is something more than just static theory. Over and over again Keynes is thinking in highly dynamic terms. Sometimes this involves brief excursions into period analysis (taking account of lags), and sometimes the analysis proceeds in terms of a moving equilibrium (continuous rates of change). And for the rest, his comparative statics is concerned not with the problems of equilibrium at one point alone but rather with the factors that cause a shift from one equilibrium position to the next. Comparative statics is in short *a* method of studying *change*.

All this is well-illustrated in Chap. 5, where he discusses Expectation as Determining Output and Employment. He begins by introducing *time:* "Time usually elapses, however—and sometimes much time—between the incurring of costs by the producer (with the consumer in view) and the purchase of the output by the ultimate consumer." The entrepreneur has to form the "best expectations he can as to what the consumers will be prepared to pay when he is ready to supply them." The modern entrepreneur, since he must produce by "processes which occupy time," has no choice but to be "guided by these expectations."[1]

These expectations fall into two groups. One class relates to the *producer*, and these may be called "short-term expectations." The second relates to the prospective returns which can be anticipated from a long-term, durable asset. These may be called "long-term expectations." Short-term expectations have to do with the outlook for *sales;* long-term expectations have to do with *investment in fixed capital*.

Keynes is here thinking in terms of period analysis. A "*change* in expectations (whether short-term or long-term) will only produce its full effect on employment over a considerable period." A lagged adjustment is here envisaged. "The change in employment due to a change in expectations will not be the

[1] All quotations in this paragraph are from the *General Theory*, p. 46.

same on the second day after the change as on the first, or the same on the third day as on the second, and so on, even though there be no further change in expectations." Thus "some time for preparation must needs elapse before employment can reach the level at which it would have stood if the state of expectation had been revised sooner." And in the case of changed long-term expectations leading to investment outlays, "employment may be at a higher level at first, than it will be after there has been time to adjust the equipment to the new situation" (pp. 47–48).

"If we suppose a state of expectation to continue for a sufficient length of time for the effect on employment to have worked itself out" completely, then the "steady level of employment thus attained may be called the long-period employment corresponding to that state of expectation" (p. 48). This is certainly a statement of interest from the standpoint of dynamics. Moreover, Keynes is careful to point out that this long-period employment once reached is not necessarily a *constant* amount. "For example, a steady increase in wealth or population may constitute a part of the unchanging expectation" (footnote, p. 48). Thus there may be a continuous rate of change.

Keynes has a good deal to say (in Chap. 5 and elsewhere) about the lags involved in the process of transition. Read in this connection what he says on pages 48 to 50. Here we have a good example of period analysis involving lagged adjustments. Changes in long-term expectations will first cause increases in the investment industries (the "earlier stages") and only later in the consumption industries (the "later stages"). "Thus the change in expectation may lead to a gradual crescendo in the level of employment, rising to a peak and then declining to the new long-period level. . . . Or again, if the new long-period employment is less than the old, the level of employment during the transition may fall for a time *below* what the new long-period level is going to be. Thus a mere change in expectation is capable of producing an oscillation of the same kind of shape as a cyclical movement, in the course of working itself out" (p. 49).

The discussion of involved lagged adjustments continues. "An uninterrupted process of transition, such as the above, to a new long-period position can be complicated in detail. But the actual course of events is more complicated still. For the state of expectation is liable to constant change, a new expectation being superimposed long before the previous change has fully worked itself out; so that the economic machine is occupied at any given time with a number of overlapping activities, the existence of which is due to various past states of expectation." Thus "the level of employment at any time depends, in a sense, not merely on the existing state of expectation but on the states of expectation which have existed over a certain past period" (p. 50).

These quotations describe precisely the kind of dynamic model that econometricians are fond of elaborating. During this complicated process of adjustment, "past expectations," he says, "have not yet worked themselves out" (p. 50).

With respect to short-term expectations there is a "large overlap between the effects on employment of the realised sale-proceeds of the recent output and those of the sale-proceeds expected from current input." But "in the case of durable goods, the producer's short-term expectations are based on the current long-term expectations of the investor" (p. 51).

Expectations play a role in all Keynes's basic functional relations. Expectations underlie the investment-demand schedule, the liquidity preference schedule, and the instantaneous multiplier. All this will be explained in later chapters, where we consider these functions in more detail. Here it is sufficient to note that Keynes's emphasis on expectations introduces a dynamic element—the difference between expected and actual rates of flow, and the difference between expected and actual stocks.

Nonetheless it is quite true that he was primarily interested in an analysis of the factors tending toward *equilibrium*, and especially in an explanation of the condition of underemployment equilibrium. This was the question that J. M. Clark had raised, namely, the "chronic limitation of production owing to limitation of effective demand."[1] Clark rightly saw, as did Keynes, that this question could not be answered by cycle theories of the type which merely stress oscillation, *i.e.*, dynamic theories of disequilibrium, which merely show how the economy sways up and down. Thus it is quite true that Keynes's primary interest was in *equilibrium* analysis. But about this, together with the related problems of statics and dynamics, we shall have much more to say in the chapters which follow.

3. INCOME (GENERAL THEORY, PAGES 52–61, 66–73)

The section on Income is of no great importance for an understanding of the *General Theory* and may quite well be omitted if the student so wishes. For those, however, who want nevertheless to know what this section is about, the following brief notes will, I trust, help to put some meaning into a discussion which many readers perhaps regard as rather useless.

It is important to call attention at the outset to the fact that the concept of "national income" has undergone a great development since 1936. Were Keynes writing his book now, he would very probably have omitted this section, making only passing reference to the path-breaking studies (in which Keynes himself played a role) on Gross National Product and National Income at Factor Cost by the British Treasury, the

[1] J. M. Clark, *Economic Reconstruction*, Columbia University Press, 1934, p. 105.

U.S. Department of Commerce, and the National Bureau of Economic Research. At the time Keynes was writing the *General Theory*, thinking on these matters had not progressed nearly so far as in recent years.[1] Thus he felt it necessary to think his way through to a clearer conception of income and costs.

He suggests three approaches to the income concept. The first is from the standpoint of total expenditures on consumers' goods and investment goods; the second is from the standpoint of the incomes of the various factors of production; the third is from the standpoint of aggregate sales minus the costs of production.

The expenditure approach can be summarized in the equation $(A - A_1) + (G' - B' - G) = Y$; the factor-income approach in the equation $F + E_p = Y$; and the sale-proceeds-minus-cost approach in the equation $A - U = Y$.

Now A is the aggregate sale proceeds received by entrepreneurs from all purchasers (consumers and entrepreneurs combined); and A_1 is the aggregate purchases by entrepreneurs from other entrepreneurs. It follows that $A - A_1 =$ consumers' purchases.

$G' - B'$ can conveniently be called G^*. Keynes's $G' - B'$ is a rather clumsy nomenclature, and I find it helpful to substitute G^* instead. G^* (that is, $G' - B'$) represents the net value of capital goods carried over from the *previous* production period before anything is spent on its maintenance and improvement.[2] It is the net value of capital inherited from the

---

[1] For standard textbooks, see in this connection J. R. Hicks, *The Social Framework*, Oxford University Press, 1942; Carl S. Shoup, *Principles of National Income Analysis*, Houghton Mifflin Company, 1947; and Richard Ruggles, *An Introduction to National Income and Income Analysis*, McGraw-Hill Book Company, Inc., 1949.

[2] B' is the amount spent on the maintenance and improvement of capital goods, and G' is what it would be worth after B' had been expended on it. Thus $G' - B'$ is the value of capital taken over from the previous period.

previous period. G is the actual value of capital equipment at
the *end* of the production period. Thus $G^* - G$ is the capital
consumption. If G (capital equipment at the end of the production period) is equal to G^* (capital equipment at the beginning of the period), then gross investment for the period in
question would just equal capital consumption; and so net
investment would be zero. If, however, G is *larger* than G^*,
then net investment in capital has occurred equal to $G - G^*$
(p. 66).

Thus if $A - A_1$ = consumers' outlays, or C, while

$$G - G^* = \text{net investment outlays, or } I, \text{ then}$$

$$(A - A_1) + (G - G^*) = C + I = Y$$

This is the first method of arriving at national income.

F is the sum paid to factors of production, and E_p (a symbol
which I find it convenient to add) is the income (*i.e.*, net
profit) of entrepreneurs. Together these equal income:
$F + E_p = Y$. This is the national income at factor cost.

Now capital consumption (that is, $G^* - G$) *plus* the purchases of materials (that is, A_1) made during the production
period will equal *user cost*, or U. Thus $(G^* - G) + A_1 = U$.
Capital consumption plus materials is the user cost of producing the aggregate goods sold (that is, A). Now the aggregate
goods sold minus user cost (capital consumption plus materials used) will equal the national income. Thus $A - U = Y$.
This is the sales-minus-cost approach.

But now we come (pp. 56-60) to the very difficult matters
relating to (1) involuntary, but not unexpected, losses and
(2) involuntary, but *also* unexpected, losses. These latter relate
to changes in market values, destruction by wars or earthquakes, etc. The former (*i.e.*, item 1 above) Keynes calls *supplementary cost*. Involuntary losses which are more or less
expected will be taken account of by the corporation or individual proprietor and debited to income account. Involuntary

and unexpected losses, however, do not enter the accounts as an *expense* but are regarded (if and when they occur) as *windfall* losses (or gains). Obviously the quite exceptional and unforeseen destruction caused by wartime bombing in Great Britain, for example, should not be deducted before arriving at aggregate national output (real income) during the war years. But *some part* of unusual or involuntary losses may reasonably be *expected*. These *supplementary costs*, which Keynes calls V, may properly be deducted in arriving at net national income. *Net* national income is thus arrived at by deducting both user cost and supplementary cost from aggregate sales, that is, $Y = A - (U + V)$.

Keynes, in his definition of depreciation (a part of his *user cost*), adopts the standard usage of the Revenue Authorities, namely, to calculate depreciation on the basis of the original cost of the equipment. This practice, indeed, makes it possible to make an unequivocal quantitative calculation of *user cost*. But it does not necessarily follow that it is good practice for economic analysis. When prices are rising, the original cost method of charging depreciation leads to an overstatement of the income produced. Indeed even for tax purposes, American corporations are allowed to value *inventories* on the LIFO (last-in first-out) method, *i.e.*, on the basis of current rather than original cost. With respect to fixed capital this is not permitted by the Revenue Authorities.

The problem of a correct calculation of depreciation is a very knotty one, and Keynes is, I believe, quite mistaken when he says (p. 60) that the concept of income which is relevant to decisions concerning current production is quite unambiguous. Indeed there is very much to be said for Hayek's thesis, criticized by Keynes, that, in order to maintain his capital, an "individual owner of capital goods might aim at keeping the income he derives from his possessions constant" (p. 60). The highly technical and complicated literature on depreciation policy and inventory valuation is sufficient to show that an unequivocal concept of business income or national income is scarcely possible. As in the case of index numbers of price movements, output, or stock of capital goods, the economist has to be satisfied with something less than perfection.[1]

4. SAVING AND INVESTMENT (GENERAL THEORY, PAGES 61–65, 74–85)

Income in the current period is defined by Keynes as equal to current investment plus current consumption expenditures. Saving in the current period is, moreover, defined as equal to current income minus current consumption. Let income be called Y, consumption C, investment I, and saving S. Then

$$Y_t = I_t + C_t$$
$$S_t = Y_t - C_t \quad \text{(that is, } Y_t = S_t + C_t\text{)}$$

Therefore

$$I_t = S_t$$

[1] In the appendix on User Cost (pp. 66–73), Keynes points out that the "short-period supply price is the sum of the marginal factor cost and the marginal user cost" (p. 67). Typically in modern theory it has been the usual practice to define short-period supply price as marginal factor cost alone. But this leaves out the purchases of materials from other firms and marginal capital consumption (*i.e.*, marginal disinvestment, p. 67). Moreover, long-period cost must include not only user cost but also "supplementary cost" and interest on loans (p. 68).

In the case of organized schemes for scrapping redundant equipment (textile machinery, for example) the *marginal* disinvestment (in value terms) is low. But marginal disinvestment (and so marginal user cost) will rise progressively as the redundancy approaches complete absorption. Thus the current supply price will rise (p. 71). This, says Keynes, is in accord with the thinking of businessmen. Economists, however, have often argued that "the disinvestment in equipment is zero at the margin of production" (p. 72). This may indeed be true "in a slump which is expected to last a long time." In general, however, a very low *marginal* user cost is likely to be a characteristic only of particular situations such as a prolonged slump, or very rapid obsolescence, or great excess capacity (pp. 72–73).

All the variables relate to the current period as indicated by the subscript t.

Investment outlays and consumption outlays are the really significant variables. "The decisions to consume and the decisions to invest between them determine incomes" (p. 64). "Saving" is a mere residual. The whole Keynesian analysis could be developed without ever using the word "saving." Indeed in the concluding sentence of Chap. 6, Keynes announced that "the conception of the *propensity to consume* will, in what follows, take the place of the propensity or disposition to save."

But Keynes in fact continued to use the word "saving" throughout his book. And in the discussion of the savings-investment problem, which followed the publication of the *General Theory*, a vast confusion arose.

One source of confusion arose from the failure of his critics to realize that while investment and saving are always *equal*, they are not always in *equilibrium*.[1] All this could have been avoided had Keynes made it clear from the outset that the *equality* of saving and investment does not mean that they are necessarily in *equilibrium*. He was realistic enough to see this, as is revealed again and again in different sections of his book. But he never explicitly stated it, doubtless because the matter had not been clearly thought through.

If the economy is in a moving equilibrium, so that the variables are always in a normal (desired) functional relationship to each other, then indeed saving and investment will not only be *equal* but will also be in *equilibrium*. But if the process of change involves a lagged adjustment of certain variables, this will not be the case. If, for example, there is an expenditure lag (*i.e.*, if consumers adjust their expenditures slowly to

[1] For a full discussion of this matter, see my Note on Investment and Saving, Appendix B, in *Monetary Theory and Fiscal Policy*, McGraw-Hill Book Company, Inc., 1949, and also my *Business Cycles and National Income*, W. W. Norton & Company, 1941, pp. 156–163.

changes in income), then, until the lag has worked itself out, *actual* consumption will not be equal to *desired* consumption (and *actual* saving will not be equal to *desired* saving). Similarly if there is an output lag, producers being slow to adjust to increases (or decreases) in sales, then unintended disinvestment (or investment) in inventory stocks will occur. Thus actual investment will diverge from *desired* (intended) investment. Under either of these conditions (expenditure lag or production lag) saving and investment, though *equal*, will not be in equilibrium. There can obviously be no *equilibrium* condition until the lags have been worked through. In equilibrium conditions (lags having been overcome) saving and investment are both *equal* and in *equilibrium*, and this is true whether the system is in moving or in stable equilibrium. But if the system is not in equilibrium, saving and investment, while still *equal*, will not be in *equilibrium*.

Now Keynes was mainly interested either in comparative statics or else in a moving equilibrium. In either case, saving and investment would be not only equal but also in equilibrium. Nevertheless, time and again in his exposition, he was dealing with an economy experiencing lagged adjustments. He could undoubtedly have developed those parts of his analysis more effectively had he clearly seen and explicitly stated that saving and investment, while always *equal*, are not always or necessarily in *equilibrium*.

It is particularly unfortunate that he did not clearly and precisely make this distinction in Chap. 7, where he in fact touches (without so stating) upon the problem of lagged adjustments in connection with his discussion of Hawtrey (pp. 75–76) and Robertson (p. 78). Hawtrey's point involved the production lag—the difference between intended investment and actual investment being unintended inventory accumulation or de-accumulation. Robertson's analysis (imperfectly stated in the *Economic Journal*, September, 1933, article cited) involved the expenditure lag—the difference between actual consumption and desired consumption.

Keynes failed in fact to face up squarely with Hawtrey's analysis, though he agreed that unforeseen changes in sales would cause actual inventory holdings to diverge from desired inventory holdings and so affect the decisions of entrepreneurs in the next production period. With respect to Robertson, the telling point is indeed made by Keynes that the Robertsonian excess of investment over saving is merely a way of saying that today's income is higher than yesterday's income. This follows from the fact that, in the article cited, Robertson confined himself to a set of definitions which can be stated in the form of equations as follows: $Y_{t-1} = C_t + S_t$, and

$$Y_t = C_t + I_t\dagger$$

The first equation means that yesterday's income Y_{t-1} is disposed of (*i.e.*, spent or saved) today. Today's saving is equal to yesterday's income minus today's consumption. The second equation means that the flow of current income springs from current consumption and current investment. It follows from these *definitions* that current income Y_t can exceed yesterday's income Y_{t-1} only if I_t exceeds S_t. These definitions, however, only establish identities. They are merely truistic statements about today's and yesterday's income. They can have no value

---

† Keynes in fact stated Robertson's definitions in an awkward manner which is likely to be confusing to the reader. In fact, the student had better strike out altogether the first sentence of the paragraph beginning at the middle of p. 78. Robertson had said quite plainly that the income spent and saved today is received on the previous day. At all events Keynes's conclusion is correct, namely, that Robertson's excess of saving over investment merely amounts to saying that income is falling.

In the article quoted by Keynes (*Economic Journal*, September, 1933), Robertson had said that income earned yesterday will be disposed of (*i.e.*, spent and saved) today. Thus the equations should be stated as follows:

$$Y_{t-1} = S_t + C_t$$
$$Y_t = I_t + C_t$$

in *analyzing* income changes. They are only descriptions of what has happened after the event.

Later, however (in his November, 1936, *Quarterly Journal of Economics* article), Robertson added a hypothesis which can be verified or disproved as a pattern of economic behavior— namely, that today's consumption is a function of yesterday's income, $C_t = f(Y_{t-1})$. But this analysis was not available to Keynes when he wrote his book. Keynes was quite correct in asserting that Robertson's article (*Economic Journal*, September, 1933) offered no *analysis*. To say that today's investment exceeded today's saving was merely a way of saying (given his definitions) that today's income exceeded yesterday's income by the same amount.

A second, but related, confusion arose because many of Keynes's critics found it difficult to reconcile the equality of saving and investment with the undeniable fact that a part of the funds going into investment often is financed from bank credit (new money) or from idle balances. How then, it was asked, could saving equal investment?[1]

The point is that, in Robertson's way of looking at the problem, the new money plus the reactivated idle balances are thought to be *in addition* to income. In the Keynesian definition the new funds, having in fact been expended in the current period, swell the current income, making it larger than it would otherwise have been. And that part of current income which is not spent on consumers' goods is in fact saved.[2] The

---

[1] Robertson (*Economic Journal*, September, 1933, p. 411) stated that his analysis corresponded to "what common-sense proclaims (even to the simple-minded) to be the essence of the matter; namely, the power possessed by the public and by the monetary authority to alter the rates of income flow—the former by putting money into and out of store, the latter by putting it into and out of existence." Thus, in his definition, $I = S + (A + B)$, in which A is new money and B is reactivated idle balances.

[2] As will be noted in Chap. 7 of this book, Pigou fully accepted Keynes's definitions.

Keynesian saving (from current income) would thus exceed Robertsonian saving (from yesterday's income). The difference between the two is the expenditure made from new money and from reactivated idle balances. Keynesian S = Robertsonian $S + (A + B)$.†

Keynes discussed this matter explicitly in an article in the *Economic Journal* of September, 1939.[1] Here he agreed that the funds available for current investment could be stated in terms of "prior saving" plus "dishoarding and credit expansion." He pointed out, however, that "the amount of saving which is taking place *at the same time* as the investment" must be exactly equal to that investment. "Saving at the prior date cannot be greater than the investment at that date. . . . Dishoarding and credit expansion provides not an *alternative* to increased saving, but a necessary preparation for it. It is the parent, not the twin, of increased saving."[2] And he concludes the argument with the following: "The rate of prior saving only tells us how much of the current investment can find a permanent home beforehand without upsetting the liquidity position and the long-term rate of interest, and without time-lag."[3]

Here it is evident that Keynes recognized the formal accuracy of the Robertsonian definitions. He noted that the Robertsonian prior saving plus dishoarding and credit creation was equal to his own current saving and also that the Robertsonian approach involved period analysis which envisaged the process of capital formation "as taking place over a period of time subject to time-lags of undetermined length."

The Keynesian way of looking at the problem appeals indeed to common sense, no less than the Robertsonian. The

† A is new money, and B is dishoarded idle balances.
[1] J. M. Keynes, "The Process of Capital Formation," *Economic Journal*, September, 1939, pp. 569–574.
[2] *Ibid.*, pp. 571–572.
[3] *Ibid.*, p. 574.

additional sales (due to the new funds thrown into the market) increase the current incomes of business units and of employed factors. Out of these enlarged current incomes, a greater saving is made. These savings are made out of income earned in the *current* period of production, and the people making these savings would not like to be told that they are not really savings. From this standpoint the definition appeals as much to common sense as the Robertsonian definition, which insists that the term "saving" must be restricted to that part of *yesterday's* income which is not currently spent on consumers' goods.

Clearly it is not a question of one definition being wrong and another being right. Anyone is free to make his own set of definitions. The only question is their usefulness. In period analysis, the Robertsonian definitions are useful and indeed necessary. In *time-rates-of-change* analysis the Keynesian definitions are appropriate. Moreover, in all countries, the Keynesian definitions are employed in the national income accounting. This is so because in national income accounts it is essential that all the variables shall apply to the same period.

Book Three

The Propensity to Consume

CHAPTER 3

The Consumption Function

[GENERAL THEORY, CHAPTERS 8, 9]

FUNCTIONAL RELATIONS AND ECONOMIC ANALYSIS

If the Keynesian system of economics consisted simply of definitional equations such as $I = S$ and $I + C = Y$, we could safely dismiss the *General Theory* from serious consideration. Economic analysis cannot make progress with such truisms as "*actual purchases* (demand) always equal *actual* sales (supply)"; nor is our understanding of the functioning of the economy deepened significantly by the proposition that "*actual* investment equals *actual* saving."

But when a demand schedule is set over against a supply schedule, we can then begin to learn something about the determination of price. Similarly with the Keynesian theory of income determination.

The student who reads widely in the critical literature on Keynes will not infrequently get the impression that the Keynesian *analysis* runs in terms of *ex post* or *realized* magnitudes. This is not correct. In the first place the Keynesian analysis takes account of expectations, as we have already pointed out[1] and shall have occasion to point out again and again. In the second place it is based on *functional relationships*. The moment *functions* (as distinct from *realized* or *observed* points in the schedules) are introduced, we are dealing with a hypothesis which can be verified or disproved as a pattern of economic behavior.

[1] See Chap. 2 in this book.

That Keynes's analysis does not run in terms of sterile ex post equations is evident at once in the opening paragraph of Chap. 8, where he resumes the argument broken off at the end of Book I. Ex post equations explain nothing; instead, Keynes begins his argument with the proposition that "the volume of employment is determined by the intersection of the aggregate supply function with the aggregate demand function" (p. 89).

The Aggregate Supply function involves few, if any, considerations not already well-known. But it is the Aggregate Demand function which has been neglected. To explain it requires an analysis of (1) the consumption function and (2) the investment-demand function. This is something very different from simply presenting the ex post equation $Y = I + C$, namely, that Aggregate Demand equals investment plus consumption.

The Aggregate Demand *function*, Keynes explains, relates any given level of employment to the expected proceeds from that volume of employment (p. 89). What the expected proceeds will be depends upon the expected outlays on consumption and the expected outlays on investment (p. 98). Accordingly it becomes necessary to analyse (1) the factors underlying consumption outlays and (2) the factors underlying investment outlays. The former involves a study of the consumption function; the latter a study of the investment-demand function.

With respect to consumption, we may consider either the function relating consumption to employment or, alternatively, the function relating consumption to real income (p. 90). In the short run, employment and real income will usually increase or decrease together more or less proportionally. But over the long run, real income tends to rise *in relation to* employment, owing to technological improvements which raise the per capita output. In the short run, however, output (real income) cannot be increased readily without an increase in employment.

Accordingly, it is a permissible and useful approach to translate the functional relation of consumer demand to employment into a functional relation of consumption expenditures (in real terms) to real income. We may therefore translate the function $D_1 = \chi(N)$ into $C = C(Y)$, where C is consumption in real terms and Y is real income. Keynes, as we have seen, deflated the nominal monetary values into real terms by means of an index of wage rates (wage units). Accordingly he writes the consumption function as $C_w = X(Y_w)$, in which the subscript w indicates that C and Y are stated in terms of wage units (p. 90).

In setting up this function, Keynes advanced the hypothesis that consumption depends primarily upon real income[1] (p. 96). Income is singled out as the main determinant of consumption just as in the case of the familiar demand curve, price is singled out as the primary determinant of the quantity taken. With respect to any such functional relation, however, it is always assumed that all other determining factors are *given and remain unchanged*. Other things remaining equal, the consumption function shows what changes can be expected in consumption from given changes in income.

The functional relation between consumption and income may be stated in the form of a schedule or table showing the aggregate amount consumed at each assumed income level; or again the relation may be presented as a curve in a diagram.

Now the curve will *shift* up (or down) if any significant change occurs in the "other factors." If any of the "other factors" change, we can say that the *parameters* of the function

---

[1] The demand for one category of consumer expenditures (namely, consumers' durables) depends very much upon the stock already acquired. Thus when the public generally is well-stocked with new automobiles and other consumers' durables, Demand will fall off even though real incomes and employment continue to remain high, owing, for example, to continued high military expenditures.

have changed. Thus an important parameter of the familiar demand curve is "consumer taste." If tastes change substantially, the demand curve for pork, for example, may rise sharply. At the same price more will be demanded than before. When any parameter of the function changes, the curve will *shift* (p. 96).

The greater part of Chaps. 8 and 9 are devoted to a consideration of the factors which underlie the consumption function and determine its *form* (*i.e.*, the *slope* and *position* of the curve). One section (pp. 91–95), however, is devoted to factors which cause *shifts* in the function.

The factors in question are classified under two broad heads, (1) the objective factors (exogenous, or external to the economic system itself) and (2) the subjective (endogenous) factors. These latter include (*a*) psychological characteristics of human nature and (*b*) social practices and institutions (especially the behavior patterns of business concerns with respect to wage and dividend payments and retained earnings) and social arrangements (such as those affecting the distribution of income).

The subjective factors "though not unalterable, are unlikely to undergo a material change over a short period of time except in abnormal or revolutionary circumstances" (p. 91). Being deeply rooted in established behavior patterns, they are likely to be fairly stable. These slowly changing factors fundamentally determine the *slope* and *position* of the consumption function and serve to give it a fairly high degree of stability. But the external factors may at times undergo rapid change and in these circumstances may cause marked *shifts* in the consumption function. We are thus concerned with two highly important matters, (1) the *form* (slope and position) of the function, and (2) *shifts* in the function.

These matters are treated by Keynes with great acumen and rich insight. But the argument is not well-arranged, and having in mind the literature which has appeared since the *General Theory*, one could easily think of many ways in which these two chapters could be improved. One must never forget, however, that, writing in 1936, Keynes was breaking quite new ground.

SUBJECTIVE FACTORS IN THE CONSUMPTION FUNCTION

Let us first consider the factors determining the *form* of the function (*i.e.*, its slope and position). The "slope" has to do with whether or not consumption rises *less* than in proportion to changes in real income, *i.e.*, whether the gap between consumption and income grows wider, as income rises, not merely absolutely, but *percentagewise* as well. Given the slope, the position still remains to be determined (*i.e.*, the "level" of the curve). In other words, what is the *amount* of consumption out of any given income, or how high is the average propensity to consume, $\frac{C}{Y}$, at any given income?

Keynes's subjective factors (pp. 107–110), as we noted above, basically underlie and determine the consumption function. We are concerned here with behavior patterns fixed by the psychology of human nature and by the institutional arrangements of the modern social order, especially the institutions which control the distribution of income.

First there are the motives "which lead individuals to refrain from spending out of their incomes." Keynes lists eight such motives. They relate to such matters as building of reserves for unforeseen contingencies; provision for anticipated future needs; the desire to enjoy an enlarged future income by investing funds out of current income, which, by yielding interest, will add to future income; the enjoyment of a sense of independence and power to do things; securing a "*masse de manoeuvre* to carry out speculation or business projects;" bequeathing a fortune; and, for some people, the satisfaction of pure miserliness.

Subjective factors (motivation) also apply to the behavior patterns of business corporations and governmental bodies. Though quite impersonal as legal entities, they are in fact only the instrumentalities through which *living human beings* act. It is sometimes said that Keynes's "psychological law" applies only to consumers. But this is not true. Moreover, he specifically included under subjective factors not only "psychological characteristics of human nature" but also "social practices and institutions" (p. 91). With respect to the behavior of business corporations and governments he listed (pp. 108–109) as motives for accumulation: (1) *enterprise*, the desire to do big things, to expand; (2) *liquidity*, the desire to face emergencies successfully; (3) *rising incomes*, the desire to demonstrate successful management; (4) *financial prudence*, the desire to ensure adequate financial provision against depreciation and obsolescence, and to discharge debt.

Keynes laid great stress on the behavior of business concerns with respect to depreciation and other reserves and noted how importantly these practices affect the amount (*level*) of consumption in relation to national income. Large financial provisions for unforeseen, though not unexpected, losses (*i.e.*, "supplementary cost") will reduce the income distributed to consumers. If such "financial provision *exceeds* the actual expenditure on current upkeep," the effect is to add to net saving and to widen the gap between consumption and income (p. 99).

In a stationary society depreciation reserves might exactly offset the replacement of worn-out and obsolete structures and equipment. But in a dynamic society which experiences business fluctuations, depreciation reserves are not always balanced by replacement investment. Following a lively investment boom in which a large number of new plants and much equipment have been constructed, replacement outlays will be very low, but the depreciation funds set aside each year will be large. These sums are abstracted from consumption in the very years when every effort should be made to strengthen consumption. New investment must be found, not only to offset the amount of net saving which individuals and corporations wish currently to make, but also to offset these newly set-up annual depreciation charges. The difficulty of finding investment outlets to offset *both* these sums may be sufficient to cause a slump (pp. 99–100).

Moreover, apart from the cycle, financial prudence may induce companies to " 'write-off' the initial cost *more* rapidly than the equipment actually wears out" (pp. 100–101). This increases net saving and widens the gap between consumption and income. Excessive sinking funds, set up by local governments and semipolitical authorities, may have the same effect (p. 100). Any "society which already possesses a large stock of capital" is confronted with the problem of accurately adjusting depreciation charges to actual capital replenishment in such a manner that the gap between consumption and income will not be abnormally widened (p. 104).

Keynes's behavior patterns are evidently not limited to consumers. His saving includes the saving of individuals, business corporations, and governmental bodies.[1] The strength of all the motives affecting saving "will vary enormously according to the institutions and organizations of the economic society" (p. 109).

These then are the psychological and institutional factors which determine both the *position* and the *slope* of the consumption function. But something more needs to be said about the normal *slope* of the curve.

---

[1] Keynes's consumption function relates consumption to national income. It is not the relation of consumption to "disposable income" as that term is defined by the U.S. Department of Commerce.

Keynes's answer to this question was highly cautious. On grounds of general knowledge and experience, he set it down as a fundamental law that *as a rule and on the average*, as income increases, consumption will increase, but not by as much as the increase in income (p. 96). With respect to the slope of the consumption function, therefore, he specified *one* (and only one) essential characteristic, namely, the marginal propensity to consume $\dfrac{\Delta C}{\Delta Y}$ must be less than unity.[1]

At this point a word of caution is necessary. Some critics have assumed that, if Keynes were right, all *historical* changes in income and consumption must conform to this rule. This is not correct. Historical changes may disclose *shifts* in the consumption function, and not simply the normal relationship between consumption and income. One must distinguish between the consumption function itself and *shifts* in the function. For example, during the Second World War, consumption in the United States fell to an abnormally low level in relation to income due to (1) inability to buy (rationing and unavailability of consumers' durables), (2) high wartime taxes, and (3) patriotic appeals to save. When the war was over, these restraints on spending were removed. Consumption under the circumstances rose rapidly in relation to income. In the transition to a more normal relation, it was *necessarily* true that consumption (starting from an abnormally low level in relation to income) should rise proportionally more

---

[1] It has been noted that the stability of the economic system depends on the rule that the marginal propensity to consume is less than unity. Were this not the case, increases or decreases in investment would have explosive effects. Note, however, Hicks's analysis in the *Trade Cycle*, Oxford University Press, 1950. For high values of the marginal propensity to consume (though less than 1) and of the accelerator, a downturn can occur when the full-employment ceiling is approached owing to the reverse action of the accelerator.

rapidly than income. During the transition period, the *increment* of consumption was absolutely larger than the increment of income. Some writers asserted that this proved Keynes to be wrong. This criticism is, however, clearly incorrect. Keynes did not say with respect to historical data, which reflects transitions from abnormal war conditions, for example, to peacetime conditions, that consumption would never rise proportionally more than income. He did say that under normal conditions, and apart from extraordinary factors which might cause *shifts* in the functional relation, some part of an absolute increase in income will be saved. In other words, the absolute increase in consumption will be less than the absolute increase in income unless extraordinary factors intervene to disturb this normal relationship.

On this *minimum* basis it is evident that consumption might rise *proportionally* as fast as income. Keynes did *not* say that consumption will rise at a rate less than in proportion to income. Thus at all income levels, consumption might be, say 90 per cent of income. Yet even on this minimum basis one important fact should not be lost sight of: If consumption rises in *proportion* to changes in income, the gap *in absolute terms* between consumption and income would widen as income increases. The *amount saved* would grow larger and larger.

There is no contradiction (as has sometimes been wrongly inferred) between Kuznets' long-run data and Keynes's fundamental law. Kuznets' data tend to show that the *per cent* of income saved (and invested) over the long run has been more or less constant at, say around 12 per cent. The *proportion* of income saved remained substantially constant. But at higher *absolute* levels of income a greater *absolute* amount was saved.

Keynes made no clean-cut distinction between the cyclical and the secular consumption function. Indeed, if we assume a *proportional* relation between income and consumption (and this comes as we have seen within Keynes's fundamental law), no distinction need be made between the *cyclical* and *secular* functions, since on this basis they would be identically the same. Such a function would start at point of origin O, as in the case of curve A in Fig. 3. On these terms the average and the marginal propensity to consume would be equal; both would be constant at a value less than unity.

All empirical evidence tends to show, however, that as income falls in the business cycle, consumption will fall proportionally *less* than income; and again when income rises cyclically, consumption will rise proportionally less than income. Secularly, however, this may not be the case.

The *secular* relation of consumption to income, in contrast with the *cyclical* relation, is a matter about which there has been a good deal of discussion, and it may therefore be useful to set out my own views as expressed in published materials in 1932, 1940, and 1941. In the 1932 reference, written several years before the *General Theory*, I suggested that, *in the long run*, consumption standards tend to rise more or less *in proportion* to increases in real income. In fact, there was nothing very novel about this: as a general tendency it is difficult to see that any economist could ever have thought otherwise. Some economists (Keynes possibly) may indeed have believed that, despite this *general* tendency, there has been *some* decline in the long-run *ratio* of consumption to income as countries have become richer. This may indeed be so, and the Kuznets data indicating a long-run constant ratio are certainly not sufficiently accurate to be conclusive. But my own thinking, rightly or wrongly, has leaned from the beginning toward the Kuznets view. In fact in the 1932 volume referred to above, I discussed this general problem very much in the manner of recent writers—namely, in terms of everyone's tendency to make his consumption standard correspond to his position in the Lorenz income-distribution curve.[1] The discussion, of course, was not cast in terms of the more rigorous consumption-function concept which Keynes developed later in his *General Theory*.

Later, however, in the chapter which I contributed to *The Structure of the American Economy*,[2] published in June, 1940, I considered both the cyclical and the secular aspects of the consumption function. The relevant passage is as follows:

> Cyclically, the percentage of income saved rises and falls as income rises and falls. If, however, one concentrates attention exclusively upon the rising secular trend in real income there is no conclusive evidence that a higher *percentage* of income is saved now than formerly. But if we save the same *percentage* of income (at corresponding phases of the cycle) as in earlier periods, it follows that the *amount* saved is higher, since real incomes have risen.

Economists have long been aware of the difference between the *cyclical* and *secular* movements of the consumption in relation to income. The Continental Cycle theorists made much of the point that the fluctuations of consumption, percentagewise, are comparatively stable, relative to income, over the cycle. But taking a longer run view, economists generally were much impressed, both from general observation and from broad studies such as those by Bowley and Stamp, with the

---

[1] See my *Economic Stabilization in an Unbalanced World*, Harcourt, Brace and Company, Inc., 1932, pp. 373, 374. For a fuller discussion of this matter, see also my *Business Cycles and National Income*, W. W. Norton & Company, 1951, pp. 164–170.

[2] *The Structure of the American Economy*, Part II, Toward Full Use of Resources, June, 1940, p. 32. This was published three months *before* Kuznets' empirical data were first presented in the Philadelphia Conference of September, 1940. This chapter was reproduced as Chap. XV of my *Fiscal Policy and Business Cycles*, W. W. Norton & Company, 1941. See also *Fiscal Policy and Business Cycles*, p. 233.

vast upsurge of consumption standards, more or less *in proportion* to the rise in income. This would not mean that consumption necessarily remains over the long run a rigidly fixed per cent of income. Indeed Kuznets' data suggest considerable variation, and of course many factors could enter to change the ratio. But even a little reflection on the course of economic history is enough to disclose the unmistakable fact that consumption has risen, broadly conceived, *more or less* in proportion to the spectacular growth in productivity which the last 150 years have witnessed.

To this general knowledge, long and widely held, Keynes indeed added something very important, namely, the precise formulation of the consumption-income schedule, together with the concept of the marginal propensity to consume. And more significant still, he developed a *theory* in which this and other functions, relevant to the determination of Aggregate Demand, are integrated. The earlier general knowledge and rather vague conceptions about the *cyclical* and *secular* behavior of consumption in relation to income did not supply a *theory*.

Keynes, as we have noted, did not clearly differentiate between cyclical movements and secular trends. It is, however, important to stress once again, in view of the widespread confusion on this matter, that Keynes's highly cautious postulate is not inconsistent with Kuznets' data.

Keynes expressed no firm conviction with respect to the short-run (cyclical) shape of the consumption function. He thought it, however, *reasonable to suppose* that consumption will as a rule rise *less* than in proportion to increases in income (p. 97). Hicks, however, has expressed the view in his *Trade Cycle* that there is no inherent reason for believing this. "I do not know any convincing theoretical reason why the proportion in which income is divided between consumption and saving should change in one way or the other with a change in income."[1] This view of the matter, if correct, would indeed be wholly consistent, as already noted, with Keynes's fundamental law. But the empirical data, and also the opinion of nearly all cycle theories over the last fifty years, is against this Hicksian suggestion. Empirical data appear to show conclusively that consumption in fact rises and falls cyclically less than in proportion to the rise and fall in real income.

Granted that such is the case, this *empirical* fact does not, however, necessarily disclose what is the *true* functional relation of consumption to income. The true function might indeed conform to Hicks's hypothesis. This hypothesis might be represented by a curve starting at the point of origin *O*. The flatter *empirical* slope *could* be explained (so it would appear) by *lags*[2] in the process of adjusting consumption to income. But this is not quite true. Lags would mean only that consumption was one or two steps behind. These lags would indeed be disclosed at the turning points. Once consumption *started* down (or up), it might, however, well move as fast, proportionally, as income. Thus the lagged adjustment could hardly explain the *slope* (*i.e.*, the crossing of the 45° line). True, the more the lag is distributed over time, the more perfectly would the lagged response qualify as an adequate explanation of the slope revealed by the empirical data.

Keynes recognized that lags *might* explain the slope of the function. He saw quite clearly that the process of adjusting consumption to income changes is likely to involve a lagged adjustment. In short periods, habits "are not given time enough" to adapt themselves to income changes. Expenditure adjustments will be made imperfectly. If income rises, saving is likely to increase at first at more than the normal rate, since consumption will for a time lag behind. If income falls, consumption will fall tardily and so saving will fall off sharply at

[1] Hicks, *op. cit.*, p. 36.
[2] *Ibid.*, Chap. III

first. All this is clearly pointed out on page 97 (first paragraph) in the *General Theory*.

Assume, however, that the slope (curve B in Fig. 3) *does* in fact represent a true functional relation (not simply lags). How may this be explained? One could argue, as Keynes suggested (last paragraph, p. 97) that *as a rule* a greater proportion of income will be saved as real income rises above the immediate primary needs of a man and his family. And on the other hand (first paragraph, p. 98), should income decline to a very low level, consumption might fall much less—indeed, being financed from reserves, might be in excess of income. Habitual behavior, based on achieved high consumption standards, would thus prevent consumption from falling proportionally as much as income. (Governmental policy, by providing unemployment relief, would moreover tend to sustain the level of consumption.) If this were the case, the empirically relatively "flat" consumption curve would represent a normal behavior pattern—a true function, and not just a lagged response to change.

In the paragraphs cited, Keynes is evidently hinting at the two leading explanations of the relatively flat cyclical consumption function conceived as a true (*i.e.*, desired or normal) pattern of behavior, not merely an expression of lagged responses to change. These two explanations are: (1) consumption is basically fixed by primary needs, and while increases in real income will indeed eventually induce increases in consumption, the urge to change consumption will not at first be in proportion to income changes; (2) consumption is basically determined by standards already achieved (*i.e.*, when income in the recent past was at its highest level). This latter point hints at what has become known in recent years as the Duesenberry hypothesis.[1] Consumption expenditure is thought

[1] James Duesenberry, *Income, Saving, and the Theory of Consumer Behavior*, Harvard University Press, 1949.

to be a function, not simply of current income, but of the highest income previously achieved. As income recedes from this level in the depression phase of the cycle, expenditure on consumption is subjected to two pulls—the former high-income standard serves to hold consumption up, while the current low income tends to pull it down. The net effect of these opposing forces is to cause consumption outlays to fall less than in proportion to the decline in income. In the recovery, as current income rises, the depressant force weakens and the pull of the formerly achieved standard becomes increasingly ascendant.

Both these explanations, I repeat, while hinted at (pp. 97, 98), are not adequately developed in the *General Theory*.[1]

Finally, there is the matter of *shifts* in the schedule. The subjective, or endogenous, factors (*i.e.*, the psychological and institutional determinants of the function) may indeed be altered as a result of "far reaching social changes" or the "slow effects of secular progress" (p. 109). Such changes could be expected to cause very gradual shifts over time in the consumption function. With these very long-run modifications Keynes was not concerned, though in occasional digressions in his argument he took account of them (p. 109). For the purpose in hand, he was prepared to "take as given the main background of subjective motives" for saving and consumption. Moreover, the distribution of wealth, being "determined by the more or less permanent social structure of the community," could also, he thought, be reckoned as "subject only to slow change over a long period" (p. 110). Thus the subjective factors which determine the normal slope and position of the consumption function were regarded by Keynes as being relatively stable.

[1] Note should be made in this connection of the brilliant work of Paul Samuelson, Arthur Smithies, Franco Modigliani, Dorothy Brady, and James Duesenberry.

OBJECTIVE FACTORS AND SHIFTS IN THE CONSUMPTION FUNCTION

But what of the objective factors? Are they not subject to changes sufficiently rapid to cause rather violent *shifts* in the consumption function?

Keynes lists six objective factors (pp. 91–95) which may under certain circumstances cause substantial shifts. Two of these may, however, be dismissed at once for reasons given in the footnote below.[1] The remaining four are as follows:

1. Windfall Gains or Losses

The phenomenal windfalls (stock-market gains) in the late twenties were generally believed to have raised the consumption of the well to do above the normal relation of consumption to income; to the extent that this was true, the consumption function was shifted upward. Until 1925 or so, consumption rose proportionally less rapidly than income. After 1925 (when the stock-market boom got under way) consumption rose roughly *in proportion* to increases in income.

---

[1] The first objective factor mentioned by Keynes is changes in the wage (and price) level. If all price and wage rates were doubled, no real changes in the relevant variables would have occurred, since all variables would tend to change *in the same proportion*. If money income were doubled (prices and wages having doubled), consumption outlays would also double. But if *real* income doubled, consumption would probably rise by less than 100 per cent.

However, changes in the value of money will already have been taken care of if the monetary values have been reduced to *real terms* by using either a price-index deflator or a wage-rate (wage-unit) deflator. Since Keynes does reduce his monetary magnitudes to *real terms*, no further consideration need be given to this factor.

The second objective factor listed by Keynes is changes in accounting practice with respect to depreciation, etc. We have considered this factor elsewhere in connection with the impact of fairly stable institutional practices on the slope of the consumption function. It is not a factor which can be thought to change violently in the short run, and it was a mistake for Keynes to include it here.

There are other possible explanations for this; and it is by no means clear how significant the windfall gains in fact were in the global national figures.

2. Changes in Fiscal Policy

The Second World War illustrates this factor in a dramatic manner. The vast war expenditures, the heavy taxation, the diversion of resources away from the production of civilian durables, the rationing and price controls—all these upset completely the normal relationship between consumption and income. The consumption function was drastically depressed below its normal level. Indeed, it may well be more accurate to say simply that all normal relationships are destroyed by the effect of upheavals of this sort. To describe such drastic changes in terms of a downward *shift* is perhaps as meaningless as to say that a great hurricane has shifted the level of the tides.

A better illustration is a major peacetime change in tax rates. Here it is certainly appropriate to speak of a downward or upward *shift* in the consumption function caused by this external (objective) factor. The modern trend toward the welfare state (financed in large part by progressive taxation), by altering the distribution of income, tends to shift upward the consumption function.

3. Changes in Expectations

A good case is the Korean War. This profoundly changed the economic outlook. Consumers anticipated future cutbacks in the production of consumer durables of all kinds. Moreover, they anticipated higher prices. There was a rush to buy. Semidurables (food and clothing) were also purchased in excess of current needs. Consumption as a ratio to current income rose. Here we could rightly say that the function was *shifted*.

4. *Substantial Changes in the Rate of Interest*

Such changes might cause a sharp fall or rise in the value of bonds and mortgages (p. 94), thereby giving rise to windfall losses or gains with effects similar to those discussed under Windfall Gains or Losses.

Apart from the effect on capital values, the effect of interest-rate changes on saving had long before the appearance of the *General Theory* been regarded as highly complex and uncertain. Keynes argues that "over a long period, substantial changes in the rate of interest probably tend to modify social habits considerably" (p. 93) but that short-period fluctuations are not likely to have much direct influence on spending.

The net conclusion with respect to the rate of interest is that short-period changes are likely to be of secondary importance. But while moderate changes in the rate of interest are not believed to cause important *shifts* in the consumption function, Keynes is careful to point out that such changes may significantly affect the *amount actually* saved. However, the effect is the opposite of what is usually believed to be the case. And the reason is as follows: A rise in rate of interest may diminish investment, and this will have the effect of reducing income. But if income falls, the *amount* saved will diminish.

General Conclusion

In general the conclusion is reached that except for quite abnormal or revolutionary changes in certain *objective* factors—expectations caused by unusual events such as wars, earthquakes, strikes, revolutions, etc.; major changes in the tax structure; quite exceptional windfall losses or gains—apart from such drastic changes, shifts in the "propensity to consume out of a given income" are not likely to be of more than secondary importance (p. 110).

We have seen above, however, that this statement does not adequately take account of the complexities involved. Yet as a first approximation, Keynes's analysis of the consumption function—the factors which cause it to *shift*, and the factors which determine its *form* (slope and normal position)—is a major landmark in the history of economic doctrines.

This principle leads to the conclusion that "employment can only increase *pari passu* with an increase in investment; unless, indeed, there is a change in the propensity to consume" (p. 98). For if the gap, in *absolute* terms, between consumption and income widens as income increases, then Aggregate Demand will not be adequate to cover the Aggregate Supply price unless that gap is filled by an increase in investment.

CHAPTER 4

The Marginal Propensity to Consume and the Multiplier

[GENERAL THEORY, CHAPTER 10]

As we shall see later in this chapter, Keynes discussed (though much too briefly) three different conceptions of the multiplier, each springing from a specific set of assumptions. These concepts are (1) the "logical" theory of the multiplier, which assumes no time lag, (2) the "period-analysis" concept of the multiplier, which assumes time lags, and (3) the "comparative-statics" timeless analysis, in which attention is concentrated on the successive points of equilibrium, the transition process being skipped entirely.

LEAKAGES AND THE MULTIPLIER

More of this later. But first let us note the comparison made by Keynes at the beginning of his Chapter 10 between Kahn's *employment multiplier*[1] and his own *investment multiplier*.

Kahn's employment multiplier is a coefficient relating an increment of primary employment (*e.g.*, on public works) to the resulting increment of total employment, primary and secondary combined. Thus if primary employment is N_2, total employment N, and k' the multiplier, then $k'N_2 = N$.

Keynes's investment multiplier, however, is the coefficient relating an increment of investment to an increment of income.

[1] R. F. Kahn, "The Relation of Home Investment to Unemployment," *Economic Journal*, June, 1931.

If Y is income and I is investment while k is the multiplier, then $kI = Y$.

Thus, to give a simple arithmetic illustration of Kahn's multiplier, if 300,000 additional men are employed in public works (including the materials used) and, as a result, employment in consumer-goods industries (secondary employment) is increased by 600,000, total employment would increase by 900,000 and the *employment* multiplier would be 3. Similarly, with respect to Keynes's multiplier, if $1,000,000,-000 additional money is spent on private construction or on public works and, as a result, expenditures on consumption should rise by $2,000,000,000, then total expenditures would increase by $3,000,000,000 and so the *investment* multiplier would be 3.

Keynes points out that the two multipliers k' and k are not identical (p. 114). *Income* in terms of wage units may rise more than employment if in the process, nonwage earners' income should rise proportionally more than wage earners' income. Moreover, under decreasing returns, total *product* would rise proportionally less than employment. In short, *income* in terms of wage units Y_w might rise, percentagewise, the most; *employment* N next; and *product* O least of all. Still, in the short run, all three—income in terms of wage units, employment, and product—would tend to rise and fall together. Thus, while not strictly correct, for practical purposes we do no great violence to the facts if we assume that the employment multiplier k' equals the investment multiplier k.[1]

---

[1] Keynes, as we have seen in Chap. 2 of this book, chose to convert investment in monetary terms into investment outlays stated in terms of wage units. As we have said above, he might advantageously have chosen to state income, investment, saving, and consumption expenditures in terms of constant dollars (*i.e.*, in terms of product or output).

If there is unused capacity of plant, equipment, and man power in consumption-goods industries, an increase in investment expenditures in money terms, by raising the income of workers and owners in the investment-goods

In business-cycle literature, the importance of the relation of an increment of investment to an increment of income (*i.e.*, Keynes's *k*) had widely been recognized, from Tugan-Baranowsky and Wicksell on. But these economists and their followers had left the matter in a vague form, being content merely to state a *tendency*. Keynes, following the lead of Kahn, supplied tools of analysis which made possible more precise thinking on this matter. The problem in hand was, as we shall see, extraordinarily complex, involving not only the *slope* and *position* of the consumption function but also *shifts* in the function. Keynes was, indeed, very cautious about placing any precise numerical value upon the multiplier. About this and related matters we shall presently have something to say. But the important thing to note here is the fact that, owing to the work of Kahn and Keynes, we are now able to attack the problem of the effect of investment on income with more precise tools of analysis than were formerly available.

The key to the analytical problem is the marginal propensity to consume. The multiplier is large or small according as the marginal propensity to consume is large or small. Once the student fully understands the implications of this statement, he will see that it throws a flood of light on a thorny problem. Indeed Kahn's June, 1931, article in the *Economic Journal* is one of the great landmarks of economic analysis.

---

industries, may cause an increase in consumption expenditures without raising prices. Real income, then, will rise. Total output will rise, not only by the amount of new investment goods produced, but also by the amount of new consumption goods produced. In *real* terms Y will have risen by the amount $I + C$. This could not happen, however, if the economy were already at full employment. At full employment an increase in investment expenditures would cause an inflation of prices unless consumption expenditures were somehow curtailed by a corresponding amount. It is therefore necessary to stress again at this point, the important fact that Keynes, in the *General Theory*, is primarily concerned with the condition of underemployment of plant, equipment and workers.

Kahn had sought to show how much secondary, or induced, employment (in consumption-goods industries) would be created if the government, for example, increased employment in public works. It is quite clear that any increase in employment in construction work and in the manufacture of materials entering into construction will increase the demand for consumers' goods and so cause an increase in *secondary* employment as a by-product of the increase in *primary* employment. This is not difficult to see. Indeed, as soon as one thinks about it, it is much more difficult to see why the "chain reaction" does not go on and on. Why does not the employment of a thousand workers lead to the employment of another thousand, and this in turn to the employment of still another thousand, until finally all workers are employed?

This indeed was a question very much debated in amateur economic discussions during the Great Depression of the thirties especially in the American cities which were considering, and in a measure experimenting with, "scrip" or "stamped-money" schemes.[1] Professional economists were, however, often not able to show precisely what was wrong with the chain-reaction line of reasoning until Kahn's famous article gave a definitive answer.

The reemployment process, Kahn explained, peters out because of *leakages*. Among the most important of these leakages are the following: (1) a part of the increment of income is used to pay off debts; (2) a part is saved in the form of idle bank deposits; (3) a part is invested in securities purchased from others, who in turn fail to spend the proceeds; (4) a part is spent on imports, which does not help home employment; (5) a part of the purchases is supplied from excess stocks of

[1] Hector Lazo, *Scrip and Barter: Their Use and Their Service*, Bureau of Foreign and Domestic Commerce. February 20, 1933; also, *Barter and Scrip in the United States*, Selected References Compiled in the Library, Bureau of Agricultural Economics, February 21, 1933.

consumers' goods, which may not be replaced. By reason of leakages of this sort, the employment process peters out after awhile. In the process, the *primary* employment has indeed induced a certain amount of secondary employment, but the amount so induced is less than one might superficially suppose.

Let us assume an initial once-for-all, nonrecurring investment expenditure[1] of $1,000,000,000 on primary employment. Let the leakages at each expenditure sequence amount to one-third of the income stream. This means that the marginal propensity to consume domestic goods is $\frac{2}{3}$. Then the total expenditures would be $3,000,000,000 including both the initial investment expenditure (primary employment) and the resulting sequence of consumption expenditures (secondary employment). This expenditure sequence is presented diagrammatically in Fig. 6.

Here it is assumed that the leakages all "run to waste." This would necessarily be true, for example, of debt repayment at the banks. Such repayment would simply cancel out a given amount of deposits. Savings, moreover, which assumed the form of hoarded currency or idle bank deposits would likewise run to waste so far as expenditures are concerned. Figure 6, in brief, represents Case I, in which the so-called leakages are indeed *true* leakages. They constitute that portion of prior income which is not spent and which therefore is lost to the income stream. Since this is the case, the income stream in-

---

[1] A matter which has given rise to misunderstanding relates to the initial expenditure. It need not be an outlay on capital goods. Keynes in fact used not only the term "investment," whether private or public, to describe the initial expenditure, but also the term "loan expenditure." This might involve funds paid out directly to consumers in the form of grants, etc., or it might involve an increase in the take-home pay resulting from tax reduction (the deficit being financed by borrowing). Whatever the initial increase in expenditure, whether private or public investment or simply an increase in private-consumption outlays resulting from tax reduction or perhaps from the spending of privately held liquid assets, the effect, as far as the multiplier process is concerned, is the same.

jected by the initial investment expenditure gradually dries up.

But now we have to consider Case II, in which the leakages, so called, are leakages only in the restricted sense that the sums involved are not spent on consumption goods. They may, however, be spent directly on investment goods. What then? In this case we had better call them simply "savings," which represent indeed leakages (*i.e.*, diversions) from *consumption* spending; but these diversions may none the less be directed

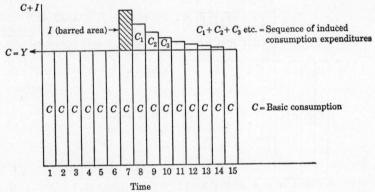

Fig. 6. The multiplier: Case I.

toward spending on investment goods. If this is done, the increment of income received in the initial expenditure period is spent *in toto* in the succeeding period, two-thirds, say, on consumption and one-third on investment. But the expenditure stream would quickly dry up were it not true that the part saved is directly expended on investment goods. This situation is represented in Fig. 7.

This leads to Case III, in which the authorities simply continue a stream of public investment expenditures amounting to $1,000,000, period after period. Here as before, in each succeeding period only two-thirds of the newly created income, we assume, is spent on consumption. In this case, that part of the income received by the public which is diverted

away from consumption is spent on bonds floated by the
government to finance a part of the continuing public investment program of $1,000,000 per period, the remaining part
being financed by (1) tapping hitherto idle balances or (2)
selling bonds to commercial banks. The total successive spendings are shown in Fig. 8.

Here a continuing stream of new investment outlays of
$1,000,000 is poured out in each successive period, and the

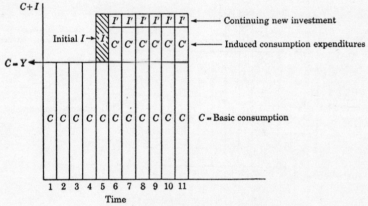

FIG. 7. The multiplier: Case II.

whole of the new saving (diversions from consumption expenditures, or leakages) is used to help finance the new investment. Eventually the new savings approximate the new investment, and so a new balance is reached. Each batch of new
investment sets going a new expenditure sequence which is
continually "running down," as can be seen by following
through any sequence of C_1, C_2, C_3, C_4, . . . , etc. It is this
"drawing off" which causes the total expenditure stream (investment plus consumption) quickly to flatten out even
though the volume of new investment is maintained at the
level of the initial injection.

In Case IV there are no leakages from consumption at all.

Here we assume again a once-for-all, nonrecurring initial investment expenditure. In this case the whole income received by workers and entrepreneurs from the initial investment outlay is spent on goods and services in the next period. This expenditure, in turn, creates new income of an equal amount, and this is spent in the succeeding period, etc. Thus the ex-

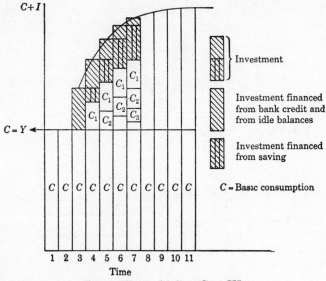

FIG. 8. The multiplier: Case III.

penditure stream, once started, continues on and on. The marginal propensity to consume being unity, there are no leakages from the consumption-expenditure stream. This is shown in Fig. 9.

In Case V we again assume a *nonrecurring* initial expenditure on investment. But here we assume that the marginal propensity to consume is zero so that the leakages drain the whole of the income derived from the initial increment of investment away from consumption; *i.e.*, the whole of the increment of income is saved. We assume further that the sums saved are not expended on investment goods; they are held as idle balances, or they are used to repay debt at banks. Thus, once the initial expenditure is completed, nothing further happens. This is illustrated in Fig. 10.

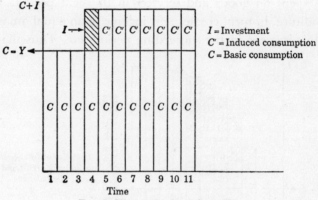

FIG. 9. The multiplier: Case IV.

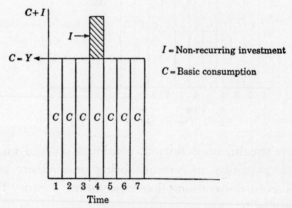

FIG. 10. The multiplier: Case V.

Finally we come to Case VI, the extreme opposite of Case V. In Case VI the marginal propensity to consume is unity, as was also true in Case IV. Here, however, we assume, as in Case III, that the initial amount of investment is maintained continuously in each succeeding period. Since the marginal propensity to consume is unity, income in each succeeding period rises cumulatively by the amount of the new continuing investment. Once full employment is reached, this situation would lead to progressive inflation. This case is presented diagrammatically in Fig. 11.

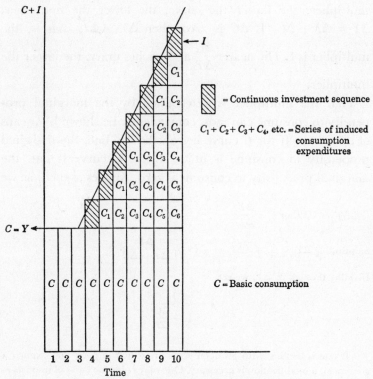

FIG. 11. The multiplier: Case VI.

From these various cases we have found that when the marginal propensity to consume is zero, the multiplier is 1; and when it is unity, the multiplier is *infinity* so that any initial increment of investment if maintained continuously will drive the economy on to inflation, as in Fig. 11. Somewhere in between is the more probable case. If the marginal propensity to consume is ⅔ (*i.e.*, if the marginal propensity to save is ⅓) the multiplier is 3. The multiplier is the reciprocal of the marginal propensity to save; $k = \dfrac{1}{1 - \dfrac{\Delta C}{\Delta Y}}$, or $k = \dfrac{1}{\dfrac{\Delta S}{\Delta Y}}$.†

The steeper the consumption-function curve, the higher the multiplier; the flatter the curve, the lower the multiplier. $\Delta Y = \Delta I + \Delta C$. If ΔC is zero, then $\Delta Y = \Delta I$; that is, the multiplier is 1. The nearer $\dfrac{\Delta C}{\Delta Y}$ approaches unity, the larger the multiplier.

That the multiplier is determined by the marginal propensity to consume can most conveniently be shown by means of diagrams. If the C curve lies on the 45° line, the marginal propensity to consume is unity. If the C curve is flat, the marginal propensity to consume is zero. Keynes argued, as we

---

† $\Delta Y = k \, \Delta I$, or $k = \dfrac{\Delta Y}{\Delta I}$

Substituting $\Delta Y - \Delta C$ for ΔI, we get $k = \dfrac{\Delta Y}{\Delta Y - \Delta C}$.

Dividing through by ΔY, we get

$$k = \frac{1}{1 - \dfrac{\Delta C}{\Delta Y}}.$$

If one is dealing with an open economy which imports and exports a good deal, a modification is necessary. One may enter the *excess* of imports as "negative investment," in which case the first figure in the expenditure series is reduced by the amount of the induced increment of *net* imports; or else one may regard the import as a leakage, in which case the term "save" in the phrase "marginal propensity to save" is arbitrarily made to include the *increment* spent on net *imports* (*i.e.*, the excess of the increment of imports over the increment of exports). If the increment of exports exceeds the induced increment of imports, the excess can be regarded as positive investment and added to the home investment figure. All this has been elaborately discussed in the vast literature on the "foreign-trade multiplier." See, for example, G. Haberler, *Prosperity and Depression*, League of Nations (Geneva), 1941, pp. 461–473, and the wealth of references there cited.

have seen (Chap. 3 of this book) that $\Delta Y > \Delta C$. This means simply that the marginal propensity to consume can in normal circumstances be assumed to be less than unity.

Kahn's analysis offered for the first time a clear answer to those who had extravagant hopes that a given increase in spending would set going a cumulative process which would of itself lead eventually to full employment. He did so by giving a precise formulation of the conditions which limit the multiplying process. The key to the answer was found in the marginal propensity to consume. If $\frac{\Delta C}{\Delta Y}$ = zero, there would be no multiple expansion, *i.e.*, the multiplier would be no more than 1. But if $\frac{\Delta C}{\Delta Y}$ is unity, then the cumulative process would continue on indefinitely. Leakages, in fact, prevent this. It was this analysis which, once and for all, disclosed why the enthusiasm of the amateur American reformers, who were sponsoring script-money spending plans in the early days of the Great Depression, was not justified. The multiplier is far smaller than they had supposed. On the other hand, it is larger than was thought to be the case by critics of the New Deal, who argued that the employment effect of public-works expenditures was limited entirely to the *initial* spending itself.

The total rise in employment will be restricted, Keynes explained, to the increase in the primary employment only "in the event of the community maintaining their consumption unchanged in spite of the increase in employment and hence in real income" (p. 117)—the case of a zero marginal propensity to consume. "If, on the other hand, they seek to consume the whole of any increment of income"—marginal propensity to consume being unity—then demand will continue to rise until full employment is reached, and thereafter "prices will rise without limit."

Thus the secondary (or multiplying) effects of any increase in investment will vary with the marginal propensity to consume. If the marginal propensity to consume is close to unity, small fluctuations in investment may cause rather violent fluctuations in income and employment; while if the marginal propensity to consume is not much above zero, very large fluctuations of investment will be needed to produce any substantial fluctuations.

It is important here to distinguish sharply between (1) the *slope* of the C curve and (2) its *position*, *i.e.*, at what level it lies. The slope might be flat, in which case the *marginal* propensity to consume would be low; at the same time there might be a very narrow spread between consumption and income at full employment income levels, *i.e.*, the *average* propensity to consume might be high. In this case, a given increase in investment (starting from a condition of unemployment) would raise income relatively little. This is true because the multiplier would under these assumptions be small. Nevertheless it might take only a rather small increase in investment to push the economy to full employment. This is true because the gap between consumption and income would, in this case, be small even at full-employment levels (see Fig. 12). Such an economy could never fall very far below full employment. Fluctuations in employment might indeed occur, but these could not be explained primarily by the multiplier; rather, they would be due to investment fluctuations—investment unaided by any significant multiplying effects.

The alternative situation, in which one assumes *both* a high marginal propensity to consume and *also* a high average propensity, is represented in Fig. 13. In this case the *fluctuation* could be very great (*i.e.*, from Y_1 to Y_F) even though the gap between C and Y is small at full-employment levels. The multiplier being very high, income would fluctuate violently if investment fluctuated even a little. At zero investment, income (contrary to the situation in Fig. 12) would be very low. Still, only a small amount of investment would produce full employment because the multiplier would be very large.

Keynes elaborates upon this matter in Sec. V, Chap. 10 (pp. 125, 126). A simple diagram would quickly have clarified the point he wished to make. But the whole is made unnecessarily difficult by a rather complicated numerical illustration. He suggests (p. 126) that the multiplier may be large in poor

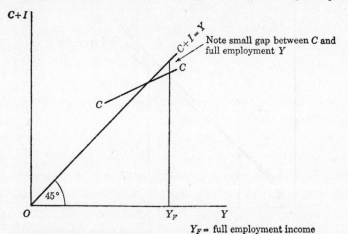

Fig. 12. High average and low marginal propensity to consume.

countries, while at the same time the *average* propensity to consume is high in such communities. This is the situation which I have represented in Fig. 13. This situation of course means not that consumption *standards* are high, but that poor communities spend a very high proportion of any increase in income and save very little even at full employment. Highly developed countries, on the other hand (p. 127), may have a relatively low *average* propensity to consume. Such a situation permits rather wide fluctuations in employment. These fluctuations would tend to be wider if a low *average* propensity (at full employment) were combined with a fairly high *marginal* propensity to consume. Such a situation is within limits possible since the slope of the *C* curve could be fairly steep even though the *position* of the curve is such that the gap between consumption and income at full employment is wide at full-employment income levels.

It would not be very difficult to improve Keynes's exposition on page 126. Still there are interesting suggestions here relating to (1) the conditions under which small fluctuations

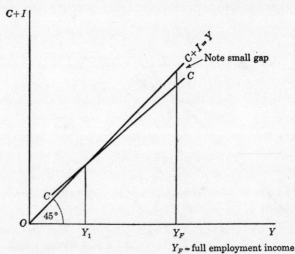

Y_F = full employment income

FIG. 13. High average and high marginal propensity to consume.

in investment will produce large fluctuations in income and (2) the conditions under which it would require large fluctuations of investment to produce large fluctuations in income and employment. The former implies a high marginal propensity to consume (hence a large multiplier); the latter a low average propensity to consume combined with a low marginal propensity to consume.

The marginal propensity to consume depends exclusively upon the *slope* of the consumption function. But the *average* propensity to consume depends partly on the *slope* and partly on the *level* or *position* of the *C* curve. Keynes is not entirely clear on this point. Note especially the last sentence on page

126. Even though we assume that a *poor* country has both a high *marginal* propensity to consume and also a high *average* propensity to consume, it could still have violent fluctuations of employment if the C function assumed the form of a straight line through the origin or is very steep as in Fig. 13. And if we arbitrarily assume that a *rich* country has a low *marginal* propensity to consume and also a low *average* propensity to consume, it *could* still experience large fluctuations in employment if investment fluctuated violently.

Keynes's fundamental law states, as we have seen, that in normal circumstances $\Delta Y > \Delta C$. On these terms the consumption function *could* be (1) a straight line through the origin, (2) a straight line crossing the 45° line, or (3) a curved line sloping off to the right. Keynes expresses the belief (p. 127) that, over the cycle, the C curve flattens out (*i.e.*, slopes to the right) as full employment is approached. If this were true, the multiplier would be relatively larger in the early stages of recovery than at the later stages of the boom. "The marginal propensity to consume is not constant for all levels of employment, and it is probable that there will be, as a rule, a tendency for it to diminish as employment increases; when real income increases, that is to say, the community will wish to consume a gradually diminishing proportion of it" (p. 120).

A large amount of unemployment is likely, he says, to be associated with negative saving in some quarters, "because the unemployed may be living either on the savings of themselves and their friends or on public relief . . . with the result that re-employment will gradually diminish these particular acts of negative saving" (p. 121). Thus when income begins first to rise, consumption may rise very little, most of the increment being applied merely to offset the former dissaving (*i.e.*, the marginal propensity to consume would be very low). Once the income rises above the "break-even"[1] point, however,

---

[1] "Break-even" here means that level of income at which net saving is zero.

a much larger part of the increase will be consumed; in other words the marginal propensity to consume will rise to a more normal level. Eventually, however, as the boom is approached, the distribution of income may become favorable to property owners (high profits) and so the marginal propensity to consume may again decline. Thus, in the first stages of advance from a *deep* depression, the multiplier may be very low, at moderately high levels of income it would tend to rise, and finally at very high levels it may again decline. Such was the view of Keynes.

But this is by no means certain. The Duesenberry thesis,[1] for example, leads precisely to the contrary conclusion.

According to Duesenberry, once a depression sets in and incomes begin to fall, it will be found, in the typical trade cycle, that the family spending unit resists any decline in consumption below the standard achieved in the recent past. Thus consumption falls proportionally less than income. Similarly, upon recovery, consumption will rise proportionally less rapidly than income until the income reached in the preceding period is again attained. At this point the former ratio of saving to income has again been regained. Once this has happened, the family spending unit is prepared to maintain this *normal* ratio of saving to income even though income should rise to levels higher than those hitherto experienced. This means that consumption now rises in the same *proportion* as income, the *ratio* remaining unchanged. But this would indicate a higher marginal propensity to consume in the high boom of the cycle. In short, during the recovery phase, until the former income level is reached, the marginal propensity to consume would be less than the average propensity; but once the former income is regained, the marginal propensity to consume would become equal to the average propensity to consume.

[1] James Duesenberry, *Income, Saving, and the Theory of Consumer Behavior*, Harvard University Press, 1949.

The consumption-income data for the boom of the twenties appear to give some support to the Duesenberry thesis. While not pretending to have discovered a general principle, I pointed out in my *Fiscal Policy and Business Cycles* (published in 1941) the following tendency: Once a fairly high income level is reached, approximately the same *proportion* of the income is consumed. "In the fairly high income years, then, about 88 per cent of the national income was consumed . . . This consumption-income pattern at relatively high income levels appears to be fairly constant." Saving, I pointed out, appears to rise proportionally more rapidly than income "at least *until the income reaches a moderately high level*."[1]

It is quite possible, however, that a special circumstance explains why consumption rose *proportionally* as rapidly as income in the last years of the boom twenties. I refer to the large speculative profits. The propensity to consume luxury goods rose to a high level owing to the unprecedented stock-market boom. Thus the statistical data showing a proportional rise in consumption relative to income may possibly (as far as the twenties are concerned) represent an upward *shift* in the consumption functions, and not the normal *shape* of the function, as suggested by the Duesenberry thesis.

Apart from the functional relation of consumption to income in the boom years of the expansion phase in contrast with the recovery years, there remains the question of whether the function may not assume one shape in the downswing of the cycle and another in the upswing. In view of the limited period for which we have reasonably good data, especially since it is necessary to exclude the violently disturbed war years, no secure conclusions with respect to this matter have as yet been reached.

[1] Alvin H. Hansen, *Fiscal Policy and Business Cycles*, W. W. Norton & Company, 1941, pp. 237, 246. The phrase quoted is not italicized in the original.

In appraising the probable expansion of employment and income from a given increment of investment, it is necessary to consider not only the magnitude of the multiplier but also possible offsetting factors which may nullify (or intensify) the original impetus. Thus a net increase in outlays on public works *may* be nullified by decreased private investment (p. 119). For example, the method of financing the public works may raise the rate of interest and so retard private investment. This unfavorable effect might be prevented if public-works policy were accompanied by an expansionist monetary policy (p. 119). Also, an increase in public works might raise the cost of capital goods and so affect private investment unfavorably. In addition, the government program might affect "confidence" unfavorably and so curtail investment. Also, public capital expenditures in an open economy might create a demand for foreign materials and foreign equipment and so help employment abroad rather than at home (p. 120). But none of these assumptions renders the multiplier analysis invalid. It is, however, true that they must all be taken into account in appraising the net effect of a given increment of public or private investment, as Keynes in fact does.

We have mentioned several times the importance of distinguishing between the *slope* of the consumption function and the *shifts* in the consumption function. The marginal propensity to consume, which may vary in different phases of the cycle and is determined by the slope of the curve, determines what the multiplier will be. But apart from the *slope* of the function, there is also the matter of *shifts* in the function. Just as it may be expected that the familiar demand function is subject to shifts (*e.g.*, changes in taste; the introduction of substitute products, etc.) so also with the consumption function.

Shifts in the function may be due to changes in taxes, temporary unavailability of consumers' durables, wartime patriotic saving, expectations of future shortages (as at the outbreak of the Korean crisis), and many other factors. Keynes was quite aware of the dynamic effect of changing expectations and changing institutions, which may cause profound shifts in the consumption function, and here and there suggestions are made in this regard in Chap. 10 of the *General Theory*.

IDENTITY EQUATIONS VS. BEHAVIOR EQUATIONS

Perhaps the most important section in Chap. 10 of the *General Theory* is Sec. IV. If this section had been carefully and sympathetically studied by Keynes's critics, very much unnecessary confusion could certainly have been avoided. Since I have canvassed the matter in some detail elsewhere,[1] I shall restrict myself here to a brief statement.

Section IV makes it evident that Keynes saw quite clearly the difference between (1) saving and investment being "equal" (identity equations) and (2) saving and investment being in "equilibrium" (behavior equations). Also he saw the difference between (1) a moving-equilibrium analysis, in which the *changing* variables are always regarded as being continuously in a "normal" relation to each other, with no time lag; (2) a step-by-step period analysis, which involves time lags; and (3) a comparative-statics analysis, which is timeless.

Identity equations, being purely tautological, explain nothing. To say that on Nov. 1, 1950, the amount of wheat purchased in the Chicago market was equal to the amount of wheat sold does not help to explain wheat prices. Similarly, as noted above identity equations such as $MV = PT$ and $I = S$ explain nothing.

[1] See my *Monetary Theory and Fiscal Policy*, McGraw-Hill Book Company, Inc., 1949, pp. 219–225, and my *Business Cycles and National Income*, W. W. Norton & Company, 1951, pp. 160–163.

Behavior equations must be sharply distinguished from mere *identity* equations. A behavior equation runs in terms of functional relations between variables. The familiar demand function is a *schedule*, relating amount demanded to price. This schedule is a statement about market *behavior*. The statement can be verified or disproved with a fair degree of accuracy by observation of the market. It is a verifiable hypothesis. Similarly with respect to the supply schedule. To say that Demand is equal to Supply is not significant. But if one says that Demand and Supply *in the schedule sense* are equal, one is saying something meaningful, namely, that if these schedules involve ranges such that they intersect, then price and quantity (purchased and sold) are mutually determined. The points of intersection become the observable (or actual) points in the two schedules. The other points are virtual points, *i.e.*, points that *might* become actual if the opposing schedules shifted appropriately. One can also say that the *virtual* points represent the *normal* or *desired* relationship of two variables. If the price is given, then people would *wish* to buy a certain amount. The demand schedule is not a schedule of *actual* prices and *actual* quantities purchased. It is a schedule stating peoples' desires. The Marshallian demand schedule represents the "propensity to buy" at different prices. Similarly the Keynesian consumption schedule represents the "propensity to consume" at different levels of income, and his saving schedule represents the "propensity to save" at different income levels.

Using schedules relating (1) the demand for investment to income, and (2) the supply of saving to income, we can readily see that income and the amount invested (or saved) would be mutually determined at the point of intersection of the two schedules.

Keynes, however, relied chiefly upon the Aggregate Demand schedule, that is, $I + C(Y)$, and the Aggregate Supply schedule to determine the level of income. Investment he regarded as determined by the marginal efficiency schedule and the rate of interest (about this, more later).[1] Given the volume of investment, so determined, and given the consumption function, these together would give us the Aggregate Demand schedule. The intersection of the Aggregate Demand schedule and the Aggregate Supply schedule would determine the level of income.

This statement, it may be pointed out, is only a first approximation since the marginal efficiency of investment schedule is not independent either of the *level* of income or of *changes* in income. Investment opportunities caused by technological developments (*i.e.*, so-called autonomous investment) can be exploited more fully at high levels of real income than would be the case at low levels of real income. Moreover, much investment is induced by *changes* in the level of income (the acceleration principle). Thus the investment-demand schedule (*i.e.*, the schedule relating investment to the rate of interest) is itself a function of income and of changes in the level of income. What is needed is a family of investment-demand schedules and similarly a family of savings schedules. From such sets of schedules, we can obtain a schedule showing the relation of income to the rate of interest, in other words, Hick's *IS* curve. To complete the picture, one needs also the *LM* curve,[2] but this matter we shall consider later in Chap. 7.

This complicated analysis requires, as we shall see, detailed discussion; but we cannot go into it here. At this point, however, let us assume, as *given*, an increment of investment and also a certain consumption function. On the basis of such data, we can then determine (as a first approximation) the increment of income by applying the multiplier analysis.[3]

[1] See Chap. 5 of this book.

[2] The *LM* curve and the *IS* curve will be explained in detail in Chap. 7.

[3] The matter is in fact more complicated since it also involves the accelerator. See my *Business Cycles and National Income, op. cit.*, Chap. 11.

THREE CONCEPTS OF THE MULTIPLIER

Now the process of expansion can be analyzed by one of three methods. All are noted by Keynes, though too briefly to ensure understanding by the reader. The first is the moving equilibrium, or "logical theory of the multiplier which holds good continuously, without time lag" (p. 122); the second is period analysis, which involves primarily a consumption-expenditure lag; the third is the comparative-statics multiplier, which is "timeless" in the sense that it leaps over the time interval between two successive static equilibrium positions. While Keynes's analysis throughout much of the chapter runs in terms of the "logical theory of the multiplier," Sec. IV in Chap. 10 is devoted mainly to the time-lag, or period, analysis. This section is therefore of particular interest since it has often either been neglected or misunderstood by critics.

Keynes begins this section by reminding the reader that the argument has been carried on up to that point on the basis of the logical theory of the multiplier, *i.e.*, the moving-equilibrium analysis, without time lag, in which it is assumed that any change in investment is foreseen so that there is no consumption-goods production lag and also no consumer-expenditure lag. In contrast, in the period analysis it is assumed that an expansion in the output of capital-goods industries is not fully foreseen. The consequences of the expansion therefore take effect gradually, subject to time lag. The full effect emerges only after an interval.

Such a lagged adjustment to an initial increment of investment can be divided into two parts, (1) a gradual increase of *investment in related industries* induced by the initial expansion, and (2) the consumption-expenditure lag. In the former case one observes "a series of increments in aggregate investment occurring in successive periods over an interval of time" (p. 123). In the latter case the consumption-expenditure lag causes

$\frac{\Delta C}{\Delta Y}$ at first to fall sharply and then in successive periods to rise again gradually to a normal ratio. Consumption rises at first less than enough to yield the *normal* relation to current income. The relation of actual consumption to *current* income is thrown out of line from the *normal* propensity to consume. Thus, says Keynes, there is a "temporary departure of the marginal propensity to consume away from its normal value, followed, however, by a gradual return to it" (p. 123).

This language has been the source of much confusion. Does the quotation just cited represent an appropriate use of the term "marginal propensity to consume"? Possibly not. A rigorous use of terms, it may perhaps be said, requires that the phrase "propensity to consume" must refer to a *normal* relationship, not to a temporary one which in fact (owing to inertia and time lag) does not correspond with normal desires. One might indeed simply say that there is a temporary departure of $\frac{\Delta C}{\Delta Y}$ away from its normal value, followed by a gradual return to it. But such a statement, while unquestionably accurate, would leave unsettled the question whether the path of $\frac{\Delta C}{\Delta Y}$ during the transition from one equilibrium position to another is subject to a verifiable behavior pattern or whether it is merely sporadic. If merely sporadic, then the statement is mere tautology; if the path follows a behavior pattern, we can speak of a true analysis of causal factors.

Precisely the same situation arises with respect to the familiar Marshallian demand and supply analysis, and here also somewhat loose language has often been used. Assume an upward shift of the demand schedule. Momentarily price will rise sharply. Suppliers cannot at once adjust themselves to the new demand situation. The "supply schedule," it has often been said, becomes momentarily inelastic with respect to price. Gradually, however, as suppliers adjust themselves to the new demand situation, the supply schedule becomes more and more elastic until it again becomes normal. Bit by bit, the supply schedule after a time lag again reaches a *normal* elasticity.

Is it appropriate in this context to use the phrase the "supply schedule"? Can the momentary inelasticity of supply with respect to price properly be regarded as a genuine *shift* in the supply schedule denoting a change in the *propensity* (*i.e.*, the short-run "normal" behavior) of suppliers? The adjustment of suppliers to the new demand situation requires *time* before a new normal supply schedule is reached. In so far as this transition behavior is systematic and verifiable, it *can* be spoken of as a "short-run normal" propensity. In this event the statement is not mere tautology.

The same terminological problem arises with respect to the theory of income determination when time lags are involved. Keynes used, as we have seen, the phrase "propensity to consume" in the same way as writers have used the phrase "short-run normal supply schedule" to explain the short-run adjustment of suppliers to a changed demand situation. If investment rises, consumers may not respond instantly to the rise in income; there is a consumer-expenditure time lag. The "marginal propensity to consume" momentarily approaches zero, or is at any rate far below "normal." But before long, consumers will adjust their expenditures so as to conform to a *normal* relation to income. The marginal propensity to consume will rise until, after a time lag, it again becomes normal. This is the way Keynes puts it.

Suppose, instead of speaking about a "propensity" (*i.e.*, a behavior pattern) we simply use an arithmetic ratio $\frac{\Delta C}{\Delta Y}$. The coefficient relating the increment of investment to an increment of income is indeed $\dfrac{1}{1 - \dfrac{\Delta C}{\Delta Y}}$, but in this context the coeffi-

cient is not based on a true propensity, *i.e.*, either a "short-run normal" or a "long-run normal" relation of consumption to income. Such a coefficient is a more *arithmetic* multiplier (*i.e.*, a truism) and not a true *behavior* multiplier based on a *behavior* pattern which establishes a verifiable relation between consumption and income. A mere arithmetic multiplier, $\dfrac{1}{1 - \dfrac{\Delta C}{\Delta Y}}$,

is tautological. The true multiplier, however, is not tautological since it is based on either a short-run normal or a long-run normal behavior pattern.

Imagine a society with a normal marginal propensity to consume of $\frac{2}{3}$. Assume we start with a stable income flow. We then inject on a sustained basis an additional 100 units of investment per year. By reason of the expenditure lag, consumption would not rise at all in the first period when the new injection is made. Let $\Delta C_1 = 0$, and $\Delta Y_1 = 100$. Then $\dfrac{\Delta C_1}{\Delta Y_1} = 0$. In the second period, $\Delta C_2 = 67$ and ΔY_2 (measured from the initial stable base) is 167; or $\dfrac{\Delta C_2}{\Delta Y_2} = \dfrac{67}{167}$. In the third period, $\Delta C_3 = 111.5$, and $\Delta Y_3 = 211.6$; thus

$$\frac{\Delta C_3}{\Delta Y_3} = \frac{111.5}{211.5}$$

In the fourth period, $\dfrac{\Delta C_4}{\Delta Y_4} = \dfrac{141}{240}$, and so on, until step by step $\dfrac{\Delta C_n}{\Delta Y_n}$ approaches the limit $\frac{2}{3}$, the normal marginal propensity to consume.

This arithmetic example illustrates Keynes's general statement quoted above. It indicates the path (based on a definite expenditure-lag behavior pattern) through which the multiplier moves during the transition period. The expenditure-lag analysis explains how the multiplier changes *during the period of transition.* "But in every interval of time the theory of the multiplier holds good in the sense that the increment of aggregate demand is equal to the increment of aggregate investment multiplied by the marginal propensity to consume," *i.e.*, the *changing* marginal propensity based on a behavior pattern, namely, a definite and predictable expenditure lag (p. 123). If indeed this is the case, we then have a verifiable behavior hypothesis which is not mere tautology.

During the transition (period analysis) the series of values of $\frac{\Delta C}{\Delta Y}$ differ (1) from the ratios which "would have been if expansion had been foreseen" (*i.e.*, the logical theory of the multiplier) or (2) the ratios which will eventually be reached "when the community has settled down to a new steady level of aggregate investment" (p. 123), *i.e.*, the comparative-statics theory of the multiplier.

It is worth stressing that it is just in the time-lag analysis that one encounters the difficult short-run-normal concept. If the time-lag theory is to escape the charge of being tautological, we must assume a short-run normal behavior pattern. No such difficulty arises either (1) with respect to the logical theory (involving instantaneous adjustment with no time lag), in which the variables of the system remain continuously in a normal relation (moving equilibrium) to each other or (2) with respect to comparative-statics analysis, which is timeless and in which the new equilibrium positions again represent a normal behavior pattern.

The moving-equilibrium analysis is the "logical theory of the multiplier, which holds good continuously, without time lag, at all moments of time" (p. 122). It assumes that a change in aggregate investment "has been foreseen sufficiently in advance for the consumption industries to advance *pari passu* with the capital-goods industries" (p. 122). If the expansion is foreseen, there will be no expenditure lag, and hence consumption will continue to hold a *normal* relation to income. Therefore, the "normal" multiplier holds good continuously. This does not mean, however, that the multiplier need necessarily be a constant. The desired ratio of consumption to income may be gradually changing, as income changes. If this is so, the normal multiplier will gradually be changing also. But there is no expenditure lag. *Desired* consumption is always equal to *actual* consumption. The system is changing over time, but it is always in equilibrium—a moving equilibrium.

It is this concept (not that of the comparative-statics analysis) that Keynes for the most part employed in this chapter.[1] That this is true is perfectly clear from the following: "The discussion has been carried on, so far, on the basis of a change in aggregate investment which has been foreseen sufficiently in advance for the consumption industries to advance *pari passu* with the capital goods industries" (p. 122), *i.e.*, on the basis of a moving equilibrium.

The timeless-multiplier, or comparative-statics, analysis simply leaps over the transition period. It skips from one equilibrium position to the next equilibrium position. It leaves out of account the time path in between. At the new equilibrium position, the increment of income (over the income of the previous equilibrium position) will be equal to the increment of investment times the multiplier (which is based on

---

[1] This point has generally been missed in the critical literature on Keynes. Critics have usually assumed that Keynes had in mind here the timeless (comparative-statics) concept. That this is wrong can be readily seen from the first sentence in Sec. IV of the *General Theory*, p. 122.

the normal propensity to consume). All during the transition (which is here left out of account), actual saving, using Keynesian terminology, is equal to investment; but only at the new equilibrium income level is *desired* saving equal to investment. In other words, the expenditure lag having at last been overcome, consumption has once again reached the *normal* or *desired* ratio to income. The timeless-multiplier analysis disregards the transition and deals only with the new equilibrium income level "when the community has settled down to a new steady level of aggregate investment" (p. 123).

Book Four

The Inducement to Invest

CHAPTER 5

The Marginal Efficiency of Capital

[GENERAL THEORY, CHAPTERS 11, 12]

Chapters 11 and 12 in the *General Theory* are exceptionally lucid and suggestive. Chapter 11, while not original, is an excellent statement of the investment-demand schedule. Here Wicksell was the pioneer, with Irving Fisher also anticipating Keynes.[1] Nevertheless Keynes contributed something, partly by making a crystal-clear statement which served to sharpen the concepts, and partly by stressing more than his predecessors the role of expectations. A contrast is made in Chap. 11 between his view of expectations and those of his predecessors, while in Chap. 12 there is a brilliant, original, and highly realistic treatment of the role of long-run expectations, *i.e.*, the role of expectations as a determinant of long-term investment.

The inducement to invest will be strong if the *Value* of an additional capital good exceeds its *Cost* (supply price or replacement cost). Now the *Value* of an additional unit of a capital good depends, on the one side, on the series of prospective annual returns which one may expect from that capital good over its lifetime and, on the other side, on the rate of interest at which these expected annual returns are discounted.

The value of a unit of capital goods can be obtained by capitalizing the series of prospective annual returns. Thus if $R_1 + R_2 + R_3 + \cdots + R_N$ is the series of prospective annual returns, or "prospective yield" of the investment, and if

[1] See my *Business Cycles and National Income*, W. W. Norton & Company, 1951, Chap. 17.

i stands for the market rate of interest, while V stands for the Value of the capital good in question, then

$$V = \frac{R_1}{1+i} + \frac{R_2}{(1+i)^2} + \frac{R_3}{(1+i)^3} + \cdots \frac{R_n}{(1+i)^n}\dagger$$

So long as the Value of a capital good (determined by the R's and the i) exceeds the supply price or Replacement Cost, which we may call C_R, of a capital good, it will be profitable to continue to invest.

The inducement to invest can equally well be stated in terms of the spread between the marginal efficiency of capital, which we may call r, and the market rate of interest i. The marginal efficiency of capital, r, can be calculated as follows:

$R_1 + R_2 + R_3 + \cdots + R_N$ being the series of prospective annual returns, or *prospective yield* of the investment, and C_R the Replacement Cost, let r stand for the rate of discount which would make the present value of the series of annual returns just equal to the supply price (replacement cost) of the capital good. Thus

$$C_R = \frac{R_1}{1+r} + \frac{R_2}{(1+r)^2} + \frac{R_3}{(1+r)^3} + \cdots + \frac{R_n}{(1+r)^n}$$

The r is the rate of discount which will equate the present *Value* of the prospective annual returns to the *Cost* of the capital good; in other words, r is the marginal efficiency of capital (Keynes) or the rate of return over cost (Fisher) which one can expect to earn on a capital asset costing C_R and yielding a series of returns represented by $R_1 + R_2 + R_3 + \cdots + R_n$.

Consider the case of a machine costing \$2,000 whose life is only three years and which offers the prospect of a series of yields of \$1,000 in each of three years. This series of \$1,000 is

† *Ibid.*, Chap. 9.

the net annual return expected from selling the output of the machine after deducting the *running* expenses (but not deducting depreciation). Or if someone else leases the machine and operates it, the series of $1,000 in each of three years is the rent obtained by the owner. Out of this rent the owner hopes to obtain enough to replace the machine plus something extra which is his return (as an absolute sum) over cost. The *rate* of return over cost (*i.e.*, the per cent r which he earns on his investment) can readily be calculated since r is the only unknown in the equation,

$$2,000 = \frac{1,000}{1+r} + \frac{1,000}{(1+r)^2} + \frac{1,000}{(1+r)^3}.$$

Within the pattern of a given set of expectations the amount of investment which is economically feasible within a given period of time will depend partly upon the elasticity of the marginal efficiency of capital schedule and partly upon the elasticity of the current supply price of capital goods (p. 136). On the one side, the diminishing marginal productivity of each successive increment of capital goods will reduce the prospective yield (series of annual returns); and, on the other side, the *cost* of a unit of capital goods will increase since a larger volume of investment will put "pressure on the facilities for producing that type of capital" (p. 136). As C_R rises while the "prospective yield" (*i.e.*, the series of R's) falls, the rate of discount (that is, r) required to equate the present value of the series of returns to replacement cost will decline. The larger the volume of investment I within a given period of time, the lower will be the prospective annual returns, *i.e.*, the R's, and the higher will be the replacement cost. Accordingly, the larger the volume of investment, the lower will be the rate of return over cost, namely, r.

The schedule relating I and r is the investment-demand schedule. Investment will be "pushed to the point on the investment-demand schedule where the marginal efficiency of capital in general is equal to the market rate of interest" (p. 137). Thus the intersection of the r curve (the marginal efficiency schedule) and the i curve (the interest-rate schedule) will determine the volume of investment within a given period of time (pp. 136–137).

The same thing can also be expressed as follows: Within a given pattern of expectations, determined basically by technological developments and population growth and in the short run by all sorts of expectations, the volume of investment in any given period of time will be determined by the intersection of the V curve and the C_R curve.

The V curve is the "demand price of investment" (p. 137), and the C_R curve is the supply price of investment, where V means the value of a unit of capital goods and C_R the replacement cost of a unit of capital goods. As investment increases within a given period of time, V falls while C_R rises. Investment will be pushed to the point on the V curve where $V = C_R$.

Keynes makes a slip on page 143, where he says that "a future fall in the rate of interest will have the effect of *lowering* the schedule of the marginal efficiency of capital." What he should have said is that a fall in the interest rate will shift the V schedule up and to the right. Thus the total investment within a given period (determined by the intersection of the V curve and the C_R curve) would rise. Alternatively, the intersection of the marginal efficiency (r) schedule with the i schedule will be at a lower point on the r curve, in view of the lower rate of interest. The resulting greater stock of capital goods means a lower marginal efficiency of capital.

Thus if the future rate of interest is likely to be lower than the present rate, a larger volume of future equipment, promising a lower rate of return over cost will offer stiff competition for today's equipment in future years. This expectation of a lower interest rate in the future may have some "depressing effect" (p. 143) upon current investment.[1]

Throughout Chap. 11 Keynes stressed the role of *expectations* with respect to the investment-demand schedule, and he concludes the chapter by emphasizing this point once again. It is mainly through the investment-demand schedule that "the expectations of the future influences the present." Static economics, he says, has made the mistake of taking account primarily of the current yield of capital equipment. But this "would be correct only in the static state where there is no changing future to influence the present" (p. 145).

Thus Keynes himself regarded his analysis as essentially dynamic. He charged that the "assumptions of the static state often underlie present-day economic theory" and this fact "imports into it a large element of unreality" (p. 146). He believed that his own emphasis on expectations, operating through the investment-demand schedule, would have the effect of "bringing it back to reality." Here, conspicuously, he failed to give credit to the important work of the Continental school of business-cycle theorists.[2]

Keynes discusses (Chap. 11) certain ambiguities with respect to the concept variously described as

1. Marginal productivity of capital
2. Marginal yield of capital
3. Marginal efficiency of capital
4. Marginal utility of capital

Which of the terms—productivity, yield, efficiency, or utility—is employed is perhaps of no great consequence. Keynes chose to use the phrase "marginal efficiency of capital" to designate the *rate of return over cost*, while reserving the phrase "prospective yield" for the *series of absolute pro-*

---

[1] Keynes might well at this point have cited Veblen's *Theory of Business Enterprise.*

[2] See my *Business Cycles and National Income, op. cit.*

spective returns from a capital good. With respect to these two quite different concepts there are certain ambiguities in the literature.

We have noted that Keynes chose to apply the term "prospective yield" to the series of annual returns derived from a capital good over its lifetime. This series of annual returns consists of the annual receipts derived from the capital good (a house rented to a tenant, for example) after deducting the running expenses *but not deducting depreciation.*

The series of absolute annual returns *could* of course be stated either way—prior to, or after, deducting for depreciation. In either case we are here concerned with a series of absolute amounts, not with a ratio (*i.e.,* a *rate* of return on an invested sum). Either of these series of absolute amounts *might* be called the marginal product of capital—the former (*i.e.,* prior to depreciation) being the "gross marginal product," and the latter (depreciation deducted) the "net marginal product." It needs to be emphasized, however, that the marginal efficiency of capital is the rate of discount which equates the gross marginal product with the replacement cost of the capital good.

Keynes calls attention to the fact that in the literature it is not always clear whether the term "marginal productivity of capital" refers to an *absolute quantity* (such as the series of absolute annual returns, whether gross or net of depreciation) or to a *ratio.* And if a ratio, it is not always made clear "what the two terms of the ratio are supposed to be." For example, one might take simply the ratio of the sum of all the series of absolute annual returns to the original cost of the capital good. One would know from this ratio that one gets, say $1,500 total returns over the lifetime of a capital good which cost, say $1,000. But that is not a very meaningful statement until one knows what the life span of the capital equipment in question is. As soon as one introduces the time element, the ratio will begin to have the "same dimension as the rate of interest" (p. 138).

As we have seen, Keynes's marginal efficiency of capital is rigorously defined as "that rate of discount which would make the present value of the series of annuities given by the returns expected from the capital asset during its life just equal to its supply price" (p. 135), in other words, that rate of discount which will make the present value of the series of prospective annual returns equal to the replacement cost of the capital good in question. Thus, over and above the cost of replacement, the sum of the annual returns is such as to yield a rate of return on the investment (*i.e.*, a rate of return over cost) equal to the indicated rate of discount. In other words, each future annual return consists of two parts, (1) discount and (2) depreciation.

The distinctive feature about Keynes's rigorous definition of marginal efficiency of capital is that he rightly takes cognizance of the entire *series* of annual "prospective yields" over the whole anticipated life of the capital good. Commonly, in discussing the marginal product of capital, economists had concentrated attention on the *current* marginal product, *i.e.*, the absolute annual product, after deducting the running expenses *and* depreciation) for the current year. In the event that the marginal product of capital was stated as a ratio, this ratio was derived by using the *net* current product (*i.e.*, deducting both running expense *and* depreciation) as the numerator and the cost of the capital good as the denominator. This would indeed give the *current* rate of return over cost. And this is in fact the method used by Marshall in the quotation appearing on pages 139 to 140 of the *General Theory*. But Keynes wished to emphasize the role of expectations over the entire series of annual products (in his terminology, "prospective yields"), and he ascertains the net return over cost throughout the *whole* anticipated life of the capital good by finding that rate of discount which makes the present value of this entire series equal to the replacement cost.

Anticipations with respect to the whole series of prospective yields from a capital asset, and not simply the expected *current* product, play a peculiarly important role for investment decisions in the case of a long-lived capital good. For such a capital good may have to compete, in its later years, with new equipment whose replacement cost is less per unit of product, or which is content (because of a then prevailing lower rate of interest) with a lower rate of return (*General Theory*, Sec. III, Chap. 11).

Finally, Keynes gives consideration (Sec. IV, Chap. 11) to the *risk* element included in the series of prospective yields. The sum of the series of annual returns must cover (1) replacement cost (depreciation),[1] (2) insurance for risk, and (3) a *pure* net "return over cost" after allowing for risk. In other words, the prospective series which is discounted should be *net* of risk if one wishes to obtain a *pure* "rate of return over cost" comparable with a pure rate of interest.

Keynes discusses in this connection two types of risk, (1) the entrepreneur's risk that the *anticipated* yields may not actually be earned, and (2) the lender's risk that the entrepreneur may default. The second risk is not involved if the entrepreneur employs his own money. But if he borrows, this risk must be added on top of the first.

Once risk is introduced, we at once encounter a very thorny problem, namely: What are the factors which determine the prospective yield of an asset? Expectations run afoul of uncertainties and risks. And Keynes turns to these mat-

---

[1] If one takes the series of absolute annual returns *net* of depreciation, one has a series similar to the annuities from a perpetual bond or consol. Discounting such a series by the appropriate rate of interest, one gets the present capitalized value of an infinite series of returns net of depreciation.

ters in his brilliant Chapter 12 on The State of Long-term Expectations.

This chapter is in line with the stream of English thinking in its emphasis on the state of *confidence* as a primary factor underlying investment decisions. But the outstanding feature of this notable chapter is the vivid picture which it gives of the "extreme precariousness of the basis of knowledge on which our estimates of prospective yield have to be made" (p. 149). These estimates, under modern conditions, are often guided as much by the expectations of those who deal on the stock market as by the more genuine expectations of the entrepreneur himself. Thus the often inscrutable waves of sentiment sweeping the stock market may make the capitalized value of the plant and equipment of a business, as reflected in the prices of its outstanding securities, less than the replacement cost of such plant and equipment. This may prevent new investment which might have been made had the more solidly grounded expectations of the true entrepreneur not been clouded by the effervescent speculations on the organized exchanges.

> We should not conclude [says Keynes] that everything depends on waves of irrational psychology . . . We are merely reminding ourselves that human decisions affecting the future, whether personal or political or economic, cannot depend on strict mathematical expectation, since the basis for making such calculations does not exist; and it is our innate urge to activity which makes the wheels go round, our rational selves choosing between the alternatives as best we are able, calculating where we can, but often falling back for our motive on whim or sentiment or chance (pp. 162–163).

CHAPTER 6

Liquidity Preference

[GENERAL THEORY, CHAPTERS 13, 15]

Money serves, we have long been told, two principal purposes, (1) as a medium of exchange, and (2) as a store of value. So at least we are told, says Keynes, referring to the second point, "without a smile on the face."[1] Actually, textbook writers on money and banking prior to the *General Theory* failed to elaborate the significance of the "store-of-value" role of money. And indeed "why should anyone outside of a lunatic asylum wish to use money as a store of wealth?"[2] Why should people desire to hold money in the form of inactive balances or "hoards"?

The answer given by Keynes is: Fear and uncertainty regarding the future. Our desire to hold a part of our resources in the form of money is a "barometer of the degree of our distrust of our own calculations and conventions concerning the future." The possession of actual cash "lulls our disquietude," and the rate of interest which we demand before we are prepared to exchange cash for earning assets is a "measure of the degree of our disquietude."[3]

The propensity to hoard is basically due to the uncertainty of our expectations, to "all sorts of vague doubts and fluctuating states of confidence and courage."[4] Liquidity

[1] See Keynes's *Quarterly Journal of Economics* article (1937), reprinted in Harris, *The New Economics*, Alfred A. Knopf, Inc., 1947, p. 187.

[2] *Ibid.*

[3] *Ibid.*

[4] See Keynes's chapter in *The Lessons of Monetary Experience*, edited by A. D. Gayer, Rinehart & Company, Inc., 1937, p. 151.

preference analysis is based on the presumption that we cannot assume a definite and calculable future. "The orthodox theory, on the other hand, is concerned with a simplified world . . . where doubt and fluctuations of confidence are ruled out, so that there is no occasion to hold inactive balances."[1] We desire to hold idle balances because we believe that such hoards serve to protect against future risk and uncertainties. In any "given state of expectation there is in the minds of the public a certain potentiality towards holding cash" (p. 205).

People can, of course, be persuaded to give up a part of their cash if the reward is great enough. The rate of interest, says Keynes, is the "premium which has to be offered to induce people to hold their wealth in some form other than hoarded money."[2] Looked at the other way round, it is worth while up to a certain point to sacrifice a certain amount of interest in order to enjoy the advantages that come from being in a liquid position. The opportunity cost of holding cash is the interest one could have earned by holding one's wealth in the form of an earning asset.

In place of the traditional twofold classification of the uses of money noted above (medium of exchange and store of value), Keynes suggests three motives for holding money, (1) the transactions motive, (2) the precautionary motive, and (3) the speculative motive. The first represents money in active circulation; the last two, money held as inactive balances. But while we can group the precautionary and speculative cash holdings together in the respect that both involve inactive balances, they cannot be classified together, as we shall see later, if we consider the factors determining the holdings.

The transactions motive relates to the need for cash for the current transactions of personal and business exchanges. The

[1] *Ibid.*, p. 151.
[2] Harris, *op. cit.*, p. 187.

precautionary motive relates to the desire to have available for future requirements and unforeseen contingencies a certain proportion of total resources in the form of cash. The amount of cash which people desire to hold in either of these two forms is only to a limited degree influenced by the cost of money (*i.e.*, the interest rate).

The speculative motive, however, relates to the desire to hold one's resources in liquid form in order to take advantage of market movements. It is the speculative motive which primarily involves the propensity to hoard. The object in view is to secure profit from knowing better than "the market" what the future may bring forth. Different individuals will estimate the prospects differently. Anyone whose opinion differs from the "predominant opinion as expressed in market quotations may have a good reason for keeping liquid resources in order to profit, if he is right" (p. 169). Thus investment counselors often advise their clients to hold, say 50 per cent of their resources in cash in order to take advantage later of a possible change in market movements. The object may be to avoid "a risk of a loss being incurred in purchasing a long-term debt and subsequently turning it into cash, as compared with holding cash" (p. 169). Thus the speculative motive for holding cash derives from a desire to keep one's resources in liquid form in readiness to take advantage of a turn in the market and to avoid a possible loss from holding securities in a falling market.

Now the *amount* of cash which people will want to hold for each of these three purposes will vary more or less with the "cost" of holding cash, namely, the rate of interest which one forgoes by holding resources in cash rather than in earning assets. Economy will be practiced in the use of cash for personal or business transactions or for precautionary purposes if the cost of cash is extremely high. But if the rate of interest is moderate, one will be prepared to sacrifice the interest for the convenience of ample liquidity (p. 168). Nevertheless, at high rates of interest even the transactions and precautionary demands for money will, to a degree, become interest-elastic.[1] At moderate or low rates of interest, the demand is likely, however, to be completely interest-inelastic. With respect to the precautionary motive, moreover, the need for cash is greatly reduced by the existence of organized security markets where one can readily dispose of bonds for needed cash (p. 170). (Thus the *amount* of cash which people will wish to hold to meet both transactions and precautionary require-ments (let us call this L') is not likely to be affected very much by the rate of interest unless this is very high.[2]) The amount of money desired for these purposes is mainly a function of the volume of payments which must be met and the contingencies, obligations, and commitments relating thereto; the amount desired will be highly inelastic with respect to the rate of interest i unless this is very high.[3]

Now while the amount of cash which people desire to hold for transactions (and precautionary) purposes is mainly a function of the volume of personal and business transactions (*i.e.*, the *trade* volume) together with the contingencies growing

[1] See my *Monetary Theory and Fiscal Policy*, McGraw-Hill Book Company, Inc., 1949, pp. 66–70.

[2] The student should note carefully that my nomenclature, in this chap-ter, differs from that used by Keynes. The first liquidity preference function (the transactions-demand function) I write as follows: $L' = L'(Y)$; Keynes wrote it: $M_1 = L_1(Y)$. The second liquidity preference function I write: $L'' = L''(i)$; Keynes wrote it: $M_2 = L_2(r)$. The total liquidity preference function as I write it is: $L = L(Y,i)$; Keynes employed the nomenclature $M = L(Y,r)$. I prefer to reserve M to mean the *quantity*, or supply, of money, while L refers to the demand for money, namely, liquidity prefer-ence. Also note that I use i for rate of interest, while Keynes used r.

[3] The "demand for money in the active circulation is also to some extent a function of the rate of interest, since a higher rate of interest may lead to a more economical use of active balances." See Keynes's chapter in Gayer's *The Lessons of Monetary Experience*, p. 149.

out of the conduct of personal and business affairs, the amount of money desired for speculative purposes (let us call this L'') is primarily a function of the rate of interest; the higher the rate of interest which one must forgo if one holds cash instead of earning assets, the less is the amount of cash which one is prepared to hold for speculative purposes. The L'' function "is a continuous curve relating changes in the demand for money to satisfy the speculative motive and changes in the rate of interest" (p. 197). The L'' function is, to a high degree, interest-elastic.

This matter—the interest-elasticity of the L'' function—is stressed very much by Keynes. It is a highly important piece in his kit of analytical tools. It plays, along with the investment-demand function and the consumption function, an important role in his attack on Say's law and the complacency of orthodox theory with respect to automatic adjustments tending toward full employment. And it is this emphasis above all else which sharply separates Keynes from the quantity theorists.

There are two ways of conceiving Say's law: (1) Say's law holds regardless of the money supply; (2) it holds only under conditions of monetary equilibrium. According to the first position, Say's law holds regardless of what monetary policy is pursued; according to the second, only in the event of an elastic monetary policy can full employment automatically be assured. Keynes denied both positions. In his attack on the second position he relied heavily on his liquidity preference analysis.

If the L'' function were not interest-elastic, open-market operations would be impracticable (p. 197). In ordinary circumstances it is always possible for banks to buy and sell bonds in exchange for cash by bidding up (or down) the price of bonds by a small amount. This means that the public can be induced to hold more (or less) cash by effecting modest changes in the rate of interest. Thus the L'' function is a "smooth curve which shows the rate of interest falling as the quantity of money is increased" (p. 171).

Uncertainty as to the future course of the rate of interest (and, as we shall see later, of prospective yields on capital assets) is the "sole intelligible explanation" of the speculative motive for liquidity which leads to holding inactive balances (p. 201). The L'' function depends primarily upon the relation between the current rate of interest and the "state of expectations" (p. 199). That the L'' schedule is a declining function of the rate of interest relates to the matter of expectations about a "safe" future rate of interest. Individuals who think that the current rate is above the safe rate (*i.e.*, who believe the bond market is too low) will not wish to hold much cash but instead will wish to hold their resources in securities. Those individuals, however, who think that the rate is too low (*i.e.*, below what they regard as the safe or probable future rate) will want to hold cash or will at least want to hold some considerable part of their resources in cash.[1] The market strikes a balance between these opposing opinions. Thus the balance of opinion with respect to the *future* rate of interest influences the *actual* rate of interest.

Those who think the prevailing rate is too low will want to hold more and more cash the wider the spread between the *actual* rate and what *they* regard as the *probable future* rate. Thus for each such individual we may assume a schedule showing the amount of cash he will wish to hold at different rates of interest in view of *his* particular expectations of the probable future rate. The summation of all such individual schedules will give the aggregate liquidity preference schedule L'' for the economy as a whole.

[1] This is true because, the rate being regarded as too low, these individuals are afraid of suffering losses if they hold their assets in the form of overpriced securities.

What is said above relates to the margin between the actual rate of interest and the probable future rate. The wider this margin, the greater will be the amount of cash which people will wish to hold. But it should also be noted that the elasticity of the L'' function is also affected by the *absolute level* of the prevailing interest rate. (The closer the rate of interest approaches zero, the greater becomes the risk of loss on capital account in holding bonds and other fixed-income assets. When the price of bonds has been bid up so high that the rate of interest is, say, only 2 per cent or less, a very small decline in the price of bonds will wipe out the yield entirely and a slight further decline would result in loss of part of the principle. The higher the price of bonds (the lower the interest rate), the smaller the "earnings from illiquidity, which are available as a sort of insurance premium to offset the risk of loss on capital account" (p. 202). Thus as the rate falls to low levels, the curve will tend to flatten out, *i.e.*, become highly interest-elastic. We learn, then, that the chief obstacle to a fall in the rate of interest to a very low level is the diminishing offset to possible loss on capital account the closer we approach a zero rate of interest. A "long-term rate of interest of (say) 2 per cent leaves more to fear than to hope, and offers, at the same time, a running yield which is only sufficient to offset a very small measure of fear" (p. 202). Liquidity preference may thus become "virtually absolute in the sense that almost everybody prefers cash to holding a debt which yields so low a rate of interest" (p. 207).[1] However, in quite abnormal circumstances this "flattening out" of the function *may* occur at a much higher rate of interest, as for example in the "crisis of liquidation" in the United States in 1932 when "scarcely

---

[1] Keynes adds here the strange and inconsistent statement that "whilst this limiting case might become practically important in future, I know of no example of it hitherto" (p. 207). In fact, the United States during the thirties (especially from 1934 on) was a good example.

anyone could be induced to part with holdings of money on any reasonable terms (pp. 207–208).

Accordingly, both the *shape* and *position* of the L'' schedule will depend upon the given "state of expectations." But a *change* in the expectations of the various individuals constituting the market will cause a *shift* in the L'' function. If market expectations point to a higher "safe" rate of interest than had previously been anticipated, the schedule will shift up or to the right. If market opinion forms a conviction that a lower rate of interest will prevail in future than had formerly been believed, the schedule will shift down or to the left.

Assuming no change in expectations, an increase in the quantity of money available for the speculative motive will lower the rate of interest by an amount fixed by the degree of interest-elasticity of the L'' function. The price of bonds can be raised sufficiently (via open-market operations) to induce some "bull" to sell his bond for cash and "join the 'bear' brigade" (p. 171). In this case we move *down* the schedule. But open-market operations, designed to increase the quantity of money, may also cause a *shift* in the schedule because such operations may give rise to "changed expectations concerning the future policy of the Central Bank or of the Government" (p. 198). But this is not certain. New developments may only cause wide differences of opinion leading to increased activity in the bond market without necessarily causing any shift in the aggregate L'' schedule. If the balance of market expectations is changed, there will be a shift in the schedule. Central Bank policy designed to increase the money supply *may* therefore be met by a shift of the L'' function, leaving the rate of interest virtually unaffected (p. 198). Thus a large increase in the quantity of money may exert only a small influence on the rate of interest in certain circumstances. Opinion about the future of the rate of interest may be "so unanimous that a small change in present rates may cause a mass movement into cash" (p. 172). "For whilst an increase in the quantity of money may be expected, *cet. par.*, to reduce the rate of interest, this will not happen if the liquidity preferences of the public are increasing more than the quantity of money" (p. 173).

On the other hand, it needs to be emphasized that *shifts* in the schedule are due to all sorts of changes affecting expectations and may have nothing to do with any changes in the quantity of money. Changes in liquidity preference schedule L'' are often confused with changes in the quantity of hoarded money. A shift in the schedule will not change the *amount* actually hoarded. The "quantity of hoards" can be changed only by changing the actual money supply or by changing the transactions demand for money, L', through changing the money income and the volume of money payments. Shifts in schedule L'' will not change the amount actually hoarded (*i.e.*, inactive balances) but will change only the rate of interest. Thus it is not true, as sometimes alleged, that "liquidity preference" is a new name for "velocity of circulation." A change in the quantity of hoards, it is usually supposed, may have a "direct proportionate effect on the price-level through affecting the velocity of circulation." But changes in the "propensity to hoard" (*i.e.*, changes in the state of liquidity preference L'') will "primarily affect, not prices, but the rate of interest."[1]

[1] See Keynes's article reprinted in Harris, *op. cit.*, p. 187. With respect to this matter, Keynes got off to a bad start in Chap. 15 (*General Theory*) by asserting that the demand for money or liquidity preference is closely connected with what is called the income velocity of money. Later he saw that this was misleading, and he sought to clarify the matter in his *Quarterly Journal of Economics* (1937) reply to Viner. Here he explained that an increase in liquidity preference (*i.e.*, a rise in the L'' function) may simply mean a higher rate of interest, not more money drawn into idle balances (*i.e.*, a decrease in velocity). The difficulty in Chap. 15, as elsewhere in the *General Theory*, is partly that he does not sufficiently distinguish between *schedules* and *observable points* in the schedules.

How changes in the quantity of money may produce changes in aggregate income (and perhaps in commodity prices) on the one side and in the rate of interest on the other depends in the first instance on the way in which changes in money come about. Suppose the money supply increases as a result of gold mining. The new gold accrues as someone's income. Or suppose the government prints money to cover its expenditures. Again the new money accrues as someone's income. The new income will largely be spent on consumers' goods, aggregate income will rise, and a part of the new money is thus needed for transactions. But some of the new money may seek an outlet in buying securities, and this will cause the rate of interest to fall. This means that some former holders of securities have been induced to sell bonds or other earning assets for cash. This money may be held as an inactive balance. Part of the new money is held for transactions purposes, and part is held for speculative purposes. Part of the new money has therefore caused a rise in aggregate income (and perhaps also in commodity prices), and a part has caused a decline in the rate of interest.

But we must leave this detour on the subject of velocity and get back on the main track—the state of expectations, liquidity preference, and the rate of interest. The state of expectations involves in fact much more than market judgments with respect to the rate of interest. Indeed expectations about the future rate of interest involve judgments about the prospective yield on capital assets in general. A holder of wealth has three alternatives. He may hold his resources in (1) cash, (2) debts, or (3) real capital assets, *i.e.*, equities. If he is more pessimistic than the market about the prospective yield on real capital assets, he will hold either cash or debts. And of these two, he will hold cash if he believes the future rate of interest will be higher than the prevailing market rate, *i.e.*, if he believes that the bond market will decline (see footnote, p. 170).

No analysis of the L'' function can be complete without introducing all three forms of wealth holding—real capital assets as well as debts and cash. In this connection a highly important supplement to the *General Theory* can be found in Keynes's *Quarterly Journal of Economics* article of 1937.[1] The analysis of liquidity preference would have been considerably improved if this material on capital assets had been included in the *General Theory*.

The three alternatives open to wealth holders—money, money loans, real capital assets—must offer "an equal advantage to the marginal investor in each of them." The prices of real capital assets must shift until "having regard to their prospective yields and account being taken of all those elements of doubt and uncertainty . . . which affect the mind of the investor, they offer an equal apparent advantage to the marginal investor" who is wavering between holding his wealth in the form of (1) a real capital asset, (2) a money loan, and (3) cash.[2]

A high propensity to hoard, given the quantity of money, will mean a high rate of interest. And given the prospective yield of a capital asset, an increase in the rate of interest will lower the price of the capital asset. Thus toward the end of a boom, the rising rate of interest will tend to dampen the rising prices of shares of common stock; but the damping effect of rising interest rates may be more than offset for a while by rising prospective yields or earnings.

Real capital assets can be newly produced. The scale on which they are produced depends upon "the relation between their costs of production and the prices which they are expected to realize in the market." Their costs on the one side and their prospective yields on the other side, together with the rate of interest at which the prospective yields are

---

[1] Reprinted in Harris, *op. cit.*, Chap. XV.
[2] *Ibid.*, p. 188.

capitalized, will determine the volume of current investment.[1]

Thus there are primarily two sets of judgments about the future (one relating to the rate of interest and the other to prospective earnings or yields) that determine the volume of investment, "neither of which rests on an adequate or secure foundation." These judgments influence the propensity to hoard. At the crisis phase of a boom there may be a "liquidity crisis," an increased propensity to hoard by reason of increased uncertainty, and at the same time a more pessimistic view about future yields. Thus there will be a movement away from *both* real capital assets (*i.e.*, equities) and bonds into cash. On the other hand, at the recovery stage of the cycle there may be a diminished propensity to hoard and at the same time a more optimistic view about future yields. Both these factors therefore tend to reinforce each other, not only at the upper but also at the lower turning point. Concretely this means that in the crisis phase a rising rate of interest (increased liquidity preference) reinforces the fall in the prospective yields of real capital assets so that on both counts the prices of capital assets are rapidly driven down, perhaps well below their costs of production. On the other hand, at the recovery stage a falling rate of interest (diminished propensity to hoard) together with a rise in prospective yields will drive the prices of capital assets above their costs of production and so will induce an increase in investment outlays and a general expansion of income and employment.

In the *expansion* phase of the cycle (*i.e.*, between the recovery phase and the crisis phase) the rate of interest is likely to rise, and this will dampen somewhat the favorable effect on the prices of real capital assets arising from the increase in prospective yields or earnings. The rise in the rate of interest reflects the fact that wealth owners, in this phase of the cycle, tend to shift from bonds and mortgages into equities. More-

[1] *Ibid.*

over, the fall in bond prices may lead to the expectation that they will fall still more, and so interest rates may be pushed still higher in a cumulative fashion.

In the contraction phase of the cycle (*i.e.*, between the crisis and the recovery) the rate of interest typically falls, and this serves to offset in a measure the unfavorable effect on the prices of real capital assets from low (and perhaps falling) prospective yields. The decline in the rate of interest reflects the fact that wealth owners, in this phase of the cycle, being pessimistic about future yields on capital assets, turn from equities to high-grade bonds (*i.e.*, fixed money claims). This raises the price of bonds and lowers the rate of interest.

Thus, to summarize, (1) in the crisis phase, a movement is likely to develop away from both equities and bonds into cash; (2) in the recovery phase, a shift occurs from cash into both equities and bonds, but predominantly into equities; (3) in the expansion phase, there is a shift from bonds into equities; and (4) in the contraction phase, there is a shift from equities into bonds.

Cash is hoarded in the crisis phase and dishoarded in the recovery phase. But what about the propensity to hold cash in the expansion and contraction phases?[1]

This indeed is a complicated matter to which Keynes gave no specific answer. But his general analysis nonetheless points the way to at least tentative conclusions. The crisis phase is the period of greatest uncertainty, and so the propensity to hoard is strongest in this phase. The recovery phase is the period of greatest calm and security, and so the propensity to hoard is least in this phase. But as the economy moves on into the boom (expansion) phase, uncertainties increase and the propensity to hoard (liquidity preference) becomes stronger and stronger. Of the three forms of wealth holding—bonds,

[1] The cycle is here divided into four phases, (1) recovery, (2) expansion, (3) crisis, and (4) contraction.

equities, and cash—bonds become increasingly undesirable as the expansion progresses; stock prices move rapidly upward until finally, months before the crisis, uncertainties and doubts begin to multiply, making it increasingly desirable to hold cash to protect against possible loss. More and more individuals will tend to shift their holdings in the direction indicated. More and more individuals become increasingly pessimistic since, as they see it, the boom is moving toward its culmination. This uncertainty and growing pessimism raise the aggregate propensity to hoard. The shift from bonds, which in the early stages of expansion moved heavily into equities, now drifts increasingly into hoards as "bear" opinion grows toward the end of a high boom. Precisely the opposite tendencies appear in the contraction phase.

Thus it is that the *propensity to hoard* is lowest in the recovery and in the early stage of expansion and highest in the crisis phase. But this does not necessarily mean that the *amount* of hoards is lowest in the recovery and highest in the crisis phase. Rather it is the rate of interest that is lowest in the recovery stage and highest in the crisis phase. What the actual *amount* of hoards will be, will depend upon the actual money supply and the relative strength of the transactions demand for money. It could well be that the boom might be carried by a wave of extreme optimism to so high a point (perhaps blown up by inflationary developments) that a very high proportion of the quantity of money is drawn into transactions use. But even in such excessively optimistic booms, there will be some wary souls who, fearful of the future, will wish to safeguard their wealth by holding cash and who will refuse to give up their liquidity even at the very high prevailing premium (*i.e.*, rate of interest). Under these circumstances, the strength of the propensity to hoard would find expression *primarily* in the high rate of interest rather than in the actual amount held as hoards.

CHAPTER 7

Classical, Loanable-fund, and Keynesian Interest Theories

[GENERAL THEORY, CHAPTER 14]

Keynes attacked the classical theory of interest on the ground that it is indeterminate.

According to classical theory the rate is determined by the intersection of the investment-demand schedule and the saving schedule—schedules disclosing the relation of investment and saving to the rate of interest (p. 175).

No solution, however, is possible because the position of the saving schedule will vary with the level of real income. As income rises, the schedule will shift to the right. Thus we cannot know what the rate of interest will be unless we already know the income level. And we cannot know the income level without already knowing the rate of interest, since a lower interest rate will mean a larger volume of investment and so, via the multiplier, a higher level of real income. The classical analysis, therefore, offers no solution.

Now exactly the same criticism applies to the Keynesian theory in its simpler form. According to the Keynesian theory the rate of interest is determined by the intersection of the supply schedule of money (perhaps interest-inelastic, if rigorously fixed by the monetary authority) and the demand schedule for money (the liquidity preference schedule). This analysis also is indeterminate because the liquidity preference schedule will shift up or down with changes in the income level. Here we are concerned with the total liquidity preference schedule including both the transactions demand and the asset demand for money. If we separate the total demand schedule for money into its two component parts, we could perhaps argue that the "pure" liquidity preference schedule (the demand for money to hold as an asset) is independent of the level of income.[1] But this does not help matters, since we cannot know, given the total money supply, how much money will be available *to hold as an asset* unless we first know the level of income and therefore how much the transactions demand for money will be. Thus the Keynesian theory, like the classical, is indeterminate. In the Keynesian case the money supply and the demand schedules cannot give the rate of interest unless we already know the income level; in the classical case the demand and supply schedules for saving offer no solution until the income is known. Keynes's criticism of the classical theory applies equally to his own theory.

Precisely the same is true of the loanable-fund theory. According to the loanable-fund analysis, the rate of interest is determined by the intersection of the demand schedule for loanable funds with the supply schedule. Now the supply schedule of loanable funds is compounded of saving (in the Robertsonian sense) plus net additions to loanable funds from new money and the dishoarding of idle balances. But since the "savings" portion of the schedule varies with the level of "disposable" income,[2] it follows that the total supply schedule of loanable funds also varies with income.[3] Thus this theory is also indeterminate.

---

[1] In fact since expectations are influenced by the level of income this is not a permissible assumption. The liquidity preference case is therefore even weaker than here indicated.

[2] "Disposable income" is here used in the Robertsonian sense, *i.e.*, yesterday's income."

[3] To make the case even stronger, it should be added that the "new money and activated balances" part of loanable funds rises and falls with increases or decreases in current income.

In the loanable-fund theory, the relevant supply schedule is conceived of in terms of loanable funds (*i.e.*, "voluntary" saving plus new money). In the analysis offered by Pigou, who adopted the Keynesian definitions, the relevant supply schedule is conceived in terms of saving out of current income. "Saving is defined as the excess of total income received over income received for services in providing for consumption."[1] Again, in the same vein, "aggregate money saving" is defined as the "excess of money income over expenditures on consumption goods."[2] Pigou's definitions are in fact, as noted above, identical to the Keynesian definitions. Money savings are that part of current income which is not consumed.

Now current income is derived from current expenditures. Whether or not current income is fed in part from the injection of new money or from the activation of idle balances makes no difference whatever from the standpoint of the Pigovian definition.[3] Income is income whether it springs from the spending of funds borrowed from banks or from the spending of "prior" income; and saving from such income is saving whether or not bank credit played a role in the process of income creation.[4]

Accordingly, in the Pigovian theory, "saving" is in effect the same thing as the so-called "loanable funds." In Robertsonian language, in fact, "loanable funds" consist of voluntary saving (*i.e.*, saving out of "disposable" income) plus borrowed bank funds and activated idle balances. In Pigovian language, saving out of current income may well exceed

---

[1] See A. C. Pigou, *Employment and Equilibrium*, 2d ed., Macmillan & Co., Ltd. (London), 1949, p. 30.

[2] *Ibid.*, p. 31.

[3] "It is important to be clear about the implications of these definitions when people or governments borrow from the banks. Everybody agrees that money so borrowed only becomes income when it is paid out, for services rendered, to factors of production" (*ibid.*, p. 30).

[4] *Ibid.*, p. 30.

"voluntary" (or Robertsonian) saving in so far as current income is increased by bank loans or the injection of idle balances. Thus the Pigovian supply schedule of *savings* amounts to the same thing as the Robertsonian or Swedish supply schedule of *loanable funds*. It is therefore not necessary to distinguish further between them, and hereafter I shall refer only to the *loanable-fund*[1] analysis on the one side and the Keynesian *liquidity preference* analysis on the other.

The neoclassical (loanable-fund) formulation and the Keynesian formulation, *taken together*, do supply us with an adequate theory of the rate of interest. From the loanable-funds formulation we get a family of loanable-fund schedules (or saving schedules in the Keynesian-Pigovian sense) at various income levels (see Fig. 14A). These together with the investment-demand schedule[2] give us the Hicksian *IS* curve (see Fig. 14B). In other words, the neoclassical formulation can tell us what the various levels of income will be (given the investment-demand schedule and a family of loanable-fund schedules) at different rates of interest. But it does not tell us *what* the rate of interest will be.

From the Keynesian formulation we get a family of liquidity preference schedules at various income levels (see Fig. 15A).

[1] The classical theory may be said to coincide with the loanable-fund theory in the special case in which no new money is being created by the banking system and in which idle balances are not being dishoarded. Classical theory (static equilibrium) assumed that saving and investment were equal *and* in equilibrium. In the Robertsonian or Swedish concept, loanable funds are equal to saving only if the system is in equilibrium; in fact, however, there may be time lags. In the Keynesian and Pigovian concepts (on this point Keynes and Pigou agreed) saving is always equal to, but not necessarily in equilibrium with, investment. But the Keynes-Pigou "saving" is always equal to the Robertson-Swedish "loanable funds."

[2] Perhaps a family of investment-demand schedules, one for each level of income. Everyone will agree that a *change* in the level of income affects the volume of investment, but not everyone will agree that the level of income is a determinant of *net* investment.

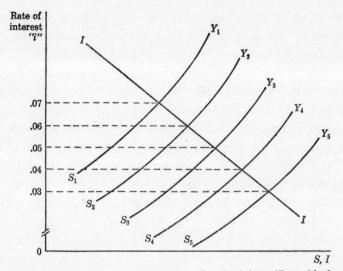

FIG. 14*A*. Family of savings schedules. *S*, schedule = "loanable-fund" schedule in Robertson's terminology, or "savings" schedule in Pigou's terminology. *Note:* Let income $Y_1 = 100$; $Y_2 = 120$; $Y_3 = 150$; $Y_4 = 200$; and $Y_5 = 260$. Then the *IS* schedule (which gives the functional relation of "*Y*" to "*I*") would be as follows:

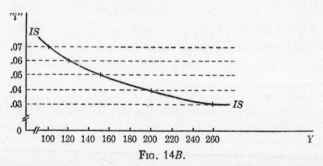

FIG. 14*B*.

These, together with the supply of money fixed by the monetary authority, give us the Hicksian *L* curve (which I prefer to call the *LM* curve)[1] (see Fig. 15*B*). The *LM* curve tells us what the various rates of interest will be (given the quantity of money and the family of liquidity preference curves) at different levels

[1] See my *Monetary Theory and Fiscal Policy*, McGraw-Hill Book Company, Inc., 1949, Chap. 5. The *LM* curve represents a situation in which $L = M$

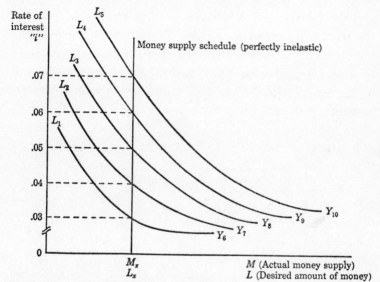

FIG. 15A. Family of liquidity preference schedules. *Note:* Let $Y_6 = 100$; $Y_7 = 155$; $Y_8 = 170$; $Y_9 = 180$; and $Y_{10} = 185$. Then the LM schedule (which gives the functional relation of "i" to "Y") would be as follows:

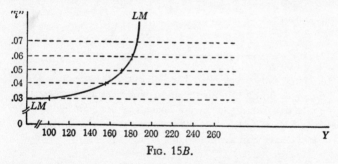

FIG. 15B.

of income. But the liquidity schedule alone cannot tell us what the rate of interest will be.

The *IS* curve and the *LM* curve are schedules relating the two variables, (1) income and (2) the rate of interest. Income

in an equilibrium sense, L meaning the demand for money and M the supply of money. Similarly the *IS* curve indicates a condition in which $I = S$ in an equilibrium sense (*i.e.*, the multiplier process has fully worked itself out).

and the rate of interest are therefore determined together at
the point of intersection of these two curves or schedules (see
Fig. 16). At this point, income and the rate of interest stand
in a relation to each other such that (1) investment and
saving are in equilibrium (*i.e.*, actual saving and investment
equal desired saving) and (2) the demand for money is in

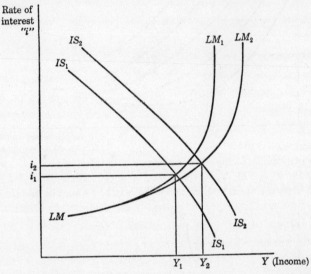

Fig. 16. *IS* and *LM* curves. *Note:* The shift of the *IS* curve from IS_1 to IS_2 is
due either to an upward shift in the underlying investment demand function
and/or to a downward shift in the saving function. The shift of the *LM*
curve from LM_1 to LM_2 is due either to an increase in the money supply
and/or to a decrease in the underlying liquidity preference schedule.

equilibrium with the supply of money (*i.e.*, the desired amount
of money is equal to the actual supply of money).

Thus a determinate theory of interest is based on (1) the
investment-demand function, (2) the saving function (or
conversely the consumption function), (3) the liquidity
preference function, and (4) the quantity of money. The
Keynesian analysis, looked at as a whole, involved all of these.
In this sense Keynes, unlike the neoclassicals, did have a

determinate interest theory. But Keynes never brought all the elements together in a comprehensive manner to formulate expressly an integrated interest theory. He failed to point out specifically that liquidity preference plus the quantity of money can give us not the rate of interest but only an *LM* curve. It was left for Hicks[1] to utilize the Keynesian tools in a method of presentation which makes it impossible to forget the whole picture, namely, that productivity, thrift, liquidity preference, and the money supply are all necessary elements in a comprehensive and determinate interest theory.

Keynes saw clearly the first part of this analysis, namely, that the classical (or neoclassical) formulation gives us no interest theory but only the *IS* curve, and in effect he stated it in these terms (p. 178). The *IS* curve is a schedule relating the two variables—aggregate income and the rate of interest. Keynes explicitly refers to this functional relationship. Given the demand curve for capital and the family of supply curves for saving, one for each income level, we can calculate the *IS* curve, since under these conditions, as Keynes put it, "the level of income and the rate of interest must be uniquely correlated" (p. 178).[2]

Having understood the first half of the story, Keynes did not, however, see that his own interest theory was equally indeterminate. He flatly asserts (p. 181) that the "liquidity preference" and the "quantity of money" between them tell us "what the rate of interest is" (p. 181). But this is not true,

---

[1] *Econometrica*, vol. 5, pp. 147–159, 1937.

[2] This proposition is again restated at the top of p. 179. But it is not true that the diagram on p. 180 in the *General Theory* closely approximates the Hicks *IS* curve. This is not true, since the multiplier must be taken account of in redrawing the whole thing on different axes—one axis being *Y*, or income, and the other being *i*, or the rate of interest. The slope of the *IS* curve will be much flatter than a curve connecting the points of intersection of the family of savings curves with the investment curve in Keynes's diagram.

since there is a liquidity preference curve for each income level. Until we know the income level, we cannot know what the rate of interest is. What we can learn from the family of liquidity preference curves and the quantity of money taken together is the *LM* curve, but this alone cannot determine the rate of interest.

That Keynes was at times confused about this is evident, for example, in the paragraph beginning at the bottom of page 183. Here he says that saving and investment are "determinates of the system, not the determinants." Now this is of course true. But in the very next sentence he includes the rate of interest as a determinant of the system along with the propensity to consume and the schedule of the marginal efficiency of capital. But this is just what is wrong. The rate of interest is, in fact, along with the level of income, a determinate and not a determinant of the system. The determinants are the three functions, (1) the saving (or conversely the consumption) function, (2) the investment-demand function, and (3) the liquidity preference function, plus (4) the quantity of money. Given these Keynesian functions and the money supply, the rate of interest *and* the level of income are mutually determined. Keynes did, however, supply the missing link (liquidity preference) needed for a determinate theory.

Lerner has suggested another method of presentation[1] (correct but less adequate, and perhaps somewhat confusing) designed to show how the three functions—marginal efficiency schedule, consumption schedule, and liquidity preference schedule—together with the supply of money, determine the rate of interest. It is an attempt to disclose the determination of the rate of interest from the intersection of two curves, (*a*) the supply of money, and (*b*) a new "sophisticated" curve which I shall label *LIS*.

[1] Abba P. Lerner, *Economics of Employment*, McGraw-Hill Book Company, Inc., 1951, p. 265.

This curve is designed to show how the total demand for money, including both the transactions demand and the asset demand, is affected by changes in income which correspond to changes in the rate of investment (account being taken of the multiplier) consistent with changes in the rate of interest. This rather complicated business can best be understood by reference to Fig. 17.

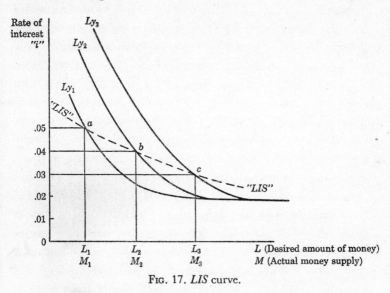

FIG. 17. *LIS* curve.

Assume three ordinary total liquidity preference schedules, L_{Y_1}, L_{Y_2}, and L_{Y_3}. L_{Y_1} is the liquidity preference schedule appropriate to income Y_1; L_{Y_2}, the schedule appropriate to income Y_2; and L_{Y_3} the schedule appropriate to income Y_3. Assume also that the income Y_1 and the interest rate of 5 per cent are appropriate to a given marginal efficiency schedule, a given consumption function, and a given money supply M_1. Assume now that the money supply changes from M_1 to M_2. This will force the rate of interest down to 4 per cent and will raise the income level to Y_2. This is true because a 4 per cent interest rate and an income level of Y_2 are the only ones consistent with the given marginal efficiency schedule, the given consumption function, the given family of liquidity preferences, and the given money supply. The amount of the rise in income will depend upon the interest elasticity of the investment-demand function and the marginal propensity to consume. The income having risen from Y_1 to Y_2, the liquidity preference schedule which will now become relevant is L_{Y_2}.

Similarly an increase in the money supply from M_2 to M_3 will reduce the rate of interest to 3 per cent, raise income to Y_3, and make L_{Y_3} the relevant liquidity preference schedule.

We may now connect up points a, b, and c to make the curve *LIS*. This is not, properly speaking, a liquidity preference schedule. It is a schedule showing the total demand for money at different rates of interest when account is taken of the various income levels which are appropriate to these different rates of interest in view of the given investment-demand schedule and the given consumption function.

It should be noted that the *LIS* curve in Fig. 17 is based on the assumption that the given investment-demand schedule and the given consumption function remain unchanged. If a shift should occur in either of these functions, these changes would produce shifts up or down in the *LIS* curve.

Thus the *LIS* curve is a peculiar hybrid. *Visible* behind it is the family of liquidity preference schedules; and *concealed* behind it are the investment-demand function and the consumption function. Thus the *LIS* curve represents an effort to subsume all three functions into one curve. This is all right so long as no one forgets all three functions. But there is a danger that someone will forget the concealed functions and begin to call the *LIS* curve a liquidity preference curve. If anyone makes this mistake, he is likely next to make the fatal error of saying that the rate of interest is determined *wholly* by liquidity preference and the supply of money, and even to assert that the marginal efficiency schedule and the savings function (or conversely the consumption function) have nothing to do with the rate of interest. Having got into this pitfall, he will even assert that a shift in the investment-demand schedule, representing an increased opportunity to invest, will have no effect whatever on the rate of interest.[1]

These are the main considerations to be deduced from Chap. 14 of the *General Theory*. In addition some interesting side issues emerge. Keynes is prepared to agree on his part that saving is an increasing function of the rate of interest (p. 178), and on the other side he presumes that the classicals would not deny that saving is a function of the income level. This is an interesting statement, and it deserves to be specially noted. Thus $S = S(i,Y)$. This could be represented diagrammatically either as a family of savings curves, one for each income level, related to the rate of interest as in Fig. 18A; or alternatively as a family of curves, one for each interest rate, related to the level of income as in Fig. 18B.

Yet while Keynes agrees that perhaps saving is a function of the rate of interest, he noted that the neoclassicals were troubled with doubts about the matter, and in fact they were not at all sure that the saving schedule was an increasing function of the rate of interest, at least within a considerable range of rates.

With respect to another subsidiary point Keynes is clearly wrong. He calls attention to the failure of the classical school

---

[1] For an example of this error see Lerner *op. cit.*, p. 106. That so lucid a writer as Lerner should fall into this error illustrates well the danger of using a formulation which does not explicitly make use of all the functions involved in the *IS* and the *LM* method of analysis. The Hicksian method makes it impossible to lose sight of all four determinants—the three functions and the money supply.

Lerner himself introduces later (p. 110) a corrective to his first narrower formulation. Nevertheless the student is likely to come away, after reading his book, with a rather narrow liquidity preference theory of the rate of interest.

to bridge the gap between the theory of the rate of interest in Book I dealing with the theory of value and that in Book II dealing with the theory of money. This is formally correct, at least with respect to many writers, but then he adds the opinion that also the *neoclassical* school had made a muddle of its attempt to build a bridge between the two. Now this certainly could not be said of Wicksell. This paragraph (p. 183) is far from convincing. The Robertsonian definition

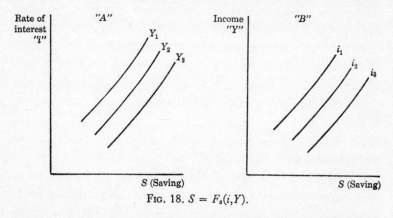

FIG. 18. $S = F_s(i,Y)$.

of saving—in effect the same concepts as were earlier employed by Wicksell and Tugan-Baranowsky—is often very useful, though for the most part the Keynesian definition[1] is to be preferred. In the terminology used by Wicksell and Robertson there are, as Keynes says, "two sources" of investment (loanable) funds, (1) "savings proper" and (2) new money and idle balances. There is surely nothing wrong with this. One needs only to be consistent in one's use of terms whatever definitions one chooses to employ, whether the Robertsonian or the Keynesian. Keynes's "muddle" charge is not valid.

On another point Keynes was on firmer ground. Besides referring to the "natural" rate of Wicksell, he also gives con-

[1] The Keynesian definition was, as we have seen, adopted by Pigou.

sideration (p. 183) to the "neutral" rate (Hayek). Wicksell's equilibrium rate was designed to maintain *price* stability, while Hayek's "neutral" rate was designed, in a progressive society, to keep *money income* stable and to drive the prices of an ever-growing volume of goods down—lower prices reflecting increased productivity. Keynes's judgment with respect to the alleged evils supposed to follow from a failure to pursue a neutral monetary policy was, I believe, sound. He averred that when it comes to neutral money "we are in deep water," and it was at this point that he dismissed the whole controversy with a stinging quotation from Ibsen's "Wild Duck." With this judgment, most economists would I believe by now agree.

Finally, Keynes makes a very important point both at the beginning (p. 177) and at the end (p. 185) of Chap. 14. He calls attention to the fact that, with respect to the matter in question, he takes a position directly opposite to that held by the classical school. The classicals held that saving automatically leads to investment. Keynes held the exact reverse, namely, that investment leads automatically to saving out of current income. The classicals had held that investment could always be increased by saving more. Keynes, on the contrary, held that investment would raise the level of income via the multiplier until additional saving was generated out of the larger income sufficient to match the new investment. Investment is thus, via the multiplier process, the main determinant of the volume of saving, not the other way round.

The corollary to all this is equally important. An increase in thrift (lower propensity to consume) may cause income to fall and so reduce the total *volume* of saving. Thus the "classical" tables are turned upside down. It is one of the great merits of the *General Theory* that, once and for all, it cleared up the muddled thinking which confused the *amount* saved with the *propensity* to save (*i.e.*, thrift).

CHAPTER 8

Nature and Properties of Capital, Interest, and Money

[GENERAL THEORY, CHAPTERS 16 AND 17]

In Sec. I, Chap. 16, of the *General Theory* Keynes continued his attack on the classical view that saving leads directly to investment. Wicksell had in fact long before stated this case, but the Wicksellian analysis had not penetrated effectively into English thinking. Keynes's challenging statement was therefore necessary. But it is often said that he overstated the case. Much saving does of course go *directly* into investment, as for instance in the building of an owner-occupant house and improvements on a farm. Keynes indeed recognized this. One motive for saving, he said (p. 108), was to carry out business projects. Again, on page 211, he admits that some saving goes *directly* into investment. Yet under modern conditions savers and real investors are to a high degree different groups.

What is really important, however, is to see clearly that an increase in the propensity to save (*i.e.*, thrift) will not increase the amount of investment. Rather, by causing a decline in consumption, income will fall. And this will cause investment to fall, and therefore the *amount* saved will decline.

On page 213 Keynes appears to argue that an increase in the propensity to save cannot affect the rate of interest. This is wrong and illustrates well the fact that he often (perhaps usually) thought that the rate of interest can adequately be explained wholly by liquidity preference and the quantity of money. This, as noted above in Chap. 7 of this book, is wrong because we never know *which* liquidity preference schedule is applicable unless we already know the level of income. If he had learned to think of the problem in terms of Hicks's *IS* and *LM* curves, he would never have asked "why, the quantity of money being unchanged, a fresh act of saving should diminish the sum which it is desired to keep in liquid form at the existing rate of interest" (p. 213). The implied answer which he expected to elicit from the reader is wrong.

Having made this introductory contact with the preceding chapters, he turns to some rather abstract considerations (in Chaps. 16 and 17) on the nature of capital. These chapters are indeed another detour which could be omitted without sacrificing the main argument. Section II opens with an argument which favors "scarcity" over "productivity" as an explanation of the value of capital. This reminds one of Cassel's "principle of scarcity" (*The Theory of Social Economy*). But the discussion is not useful. "Scarcity" has no economic meaning except in so far as it determines what point of a marginal-productivity schedule will become the "observable" point. "If capital becomes less scarce, the excess yield will diminish" (p. 213), which means, contrary to what Keynes says, that it is less productive.[1]

Keynes's flat statement (p. 213) that he finds sympathy with the "preclassical" doctrine that everything is "produced by labour" aided by technique, natural resources, and "past labour, embodied in assets," has often been cited as a pronouncement in support of the labor theory of value. "It is preferable to regard labour, including, of course, the personal

[1] One could perhaps make some sense out of his statement that it would at least not become less productive in a physical sense by applying his analysis to housing. If the stock of houses increases, their yield (*i.e.*, annual rentals) will fall but the physical housing facilities provided by the hundredth house of identical size and quality is the same as that provided by the fiftieth house.

services of the entrepreneur and his assistants, as the sole factor of production, operating in a given environment of technique, natural resources, capital equipment and effective demand" (pp. 213–214). Labor, money, and time, he says, are the only physical units he needs for his analysis. But does this mean that he adheres to the labor theory of value? Certainly not. It is one thing to use "labour-units" as an instrument of measurement and quite another thing to make labor the sole determinant of value.

Keynes argues that capital has value because it is scarce. And it is scarce because capital involves lengthy or roundabout processes.[1] It is the roundaboutness of the process that keeps capital sufficiently scarce so that the sum of its anticipated future yields (annual earnings or rentals) will exceed the cost of production. In other words, the roundabout process—the capital-using method—will not be undertaken unless the anticipated proceeds exceed those from the direct application of labor. Thus if the rate of interest exceeds zero, a "new element of cost is introduced which increases with the length of the process" (p. 216). Accordingly the supply of capital will be curtailed until the prospective annual yields have "increased sufficiently to cover the increased cost" (p. 216). Capital has to be kept scarce enough "to have a marginal efficiency which is at least equal to the rate of interest" (p. 217). This is surely not a labor theory of value.

But now suppose (1) a society "so well equipped with capital that its marginal efficiency is zero" (p. 217), yet possessing a monetary system such that money will "keep,"

---

[1] Keynes argues (p. 215) that there are other reasons why capital is scarce, including disagreeable attendant circumstances such as "smelly or risky" processes. But this reasoning is not valid, since such disagreeable attendant circumstances also apply to direct production processes. It is the roundaboutness of the capital-using process that makes it sufficiently scarce so that the sum of its anticipated yields will exceed its replacement cost.

costs of storage being negligible, and (2) a society disposed to save in conditions of full employment even at a zero rate of interest. Entrepreneurs will in these circumstances make losses if they attempt to offer full employment by making capital outlays offsetting the net savings.[1] These losses will cause employment to fall until income drops low enough "to bring savings to zero" (p. 218). The alternative would be a situation in which "the aggregate desire on the part of the public to make provision for the future" (p. 218) was sufficiently satiated so that they would save nothing at a full-employment income.[2]

Now assume "an institutional factor" in the form of money which prevents the rate of interest from being negative (p. 218). In fact institutional and psychological factors "set a limit much above zero" since in addition to uncertainty as to the future (*i.e.*, the pure rate) there are also the "costs of bringing borrowers and lenders together" (p. 219). The lower limit may thus be not zero, but "2 or 2½ per cent on long-term" (p. 219). When the stock of capital becomes so large that the marginal efficiency of capital reaches this minimum rate of interest, net investment will cease, and employment and income will decline until saving is also reduced to zero.

This situation, says Keynes, seems to describe the experiences of Great Britain and the United States in the interwar period (p. 219). A community with a smaller stock of capital (but with the same technique) and therefore with a higher marginal efficiency of capital may thus enjoy more investment and a higher level of income and employment

---

[1] This is true because, in view of the existing large stock of capital, the rate of return on net investment would be less than the rate of interest. Thus an effort to invest all the savings potentially available at full employment would cause losses.

[2] This section of the *General Theory* is badly written.

than one so satiated with capital that the marginal efficiency of capital has been driven down to, or even below, the minimum rate of interest. The community rich in capital goods is worse off than the poorer community in the sense that the former may suffer from unemployment, while the latter with large, untapped investment opportunities may experience full employment. There is of course nothing very paradoxical about what Keynes says here. We have long known, for example, that a community is relatively rich in its stock of capital goods at the end of a boom. Satiated with fixed capital, investment falls; unemployment and depression ensue.

Suppose now "State action enters as a balancing factor" so that the "growth of capital equipment" continues (with a declining rate of interest) until the marginal efficiency of capital is brought down to zero. We should then have reached a state of "full investment" in which there is no interest cost and in which "the products of capital" would be "selling at a price proportioned to the labour, etc., embodied in them" (p. 221). Then indeed we should have reached (apart from the rent value of scarce natural resources) a labor theory of value.

Keynes's views here resemble very much the utopian St.-Simonians of the early nineteenth century who laid great stress on the rewards of enterprise but minimized the rewards of accumulated wealth. "Though the rentier would disappear, there would still be room, nevertheless, for enterprise and skill" (p. 221). Indeed so far as wealth ownership is concerned, there would still be, even though the pure rate of interest were zero, a "gross yield of assets including the return in respect of risk" (p. 221).

Thus we find Keynes permitting himself in Chap. 16 a free range of speculation about an economy in which the marginal efficiency of capital, and presumably also the rate of interest, is somehow (the method is not clearly disclosed) driven down to zero. Elsewhere, in Chaps. 15 and 17, and even in parts of

Chap. 16 itself, he presents institutional grounds for believing that the rate of interest cannot fall below a certain minimum. The "rentier euthanasia" discussion is a kind of "free-wheeling" detour by Keynes in his less responsible moments.

All this was written in times of peace when Keynes, perhaps naïvely, was looking forward to a continued peaceful world. The war and its aftermath, with its capital shortages and inflationary pressures, have profoundly changed the interest-rate picture. Keynes was well aware of these fundamental changes before he died.[1] Practical policies must be adapted to changed conditions. Keynes's basic theoretical structure stands on its own and is not *as such* involved in some of the vague speculations contained in this chapter. Moreover, with respect to practical policies, his theoretical *analysis* can be applied to capital shortage and inflationary conditions as well as to the problems of underemployment.

Chapter 17, on the properties of interest and money, ties in with the subject matter of money and liquidity preference— the themes of Chaps. 13 and 15. But the topic is elevated to a very abstract plane. Immediately after the appearance of the *General Theory* there was a certain fascination about Chap. 17, due partly no doubt to its obscurity. Digging in this area, however, soon ceased after it was found that the chapter contained no gold mines. Still the discussion (though it certainly could be improved) is not altogether without merit, and some interesting bits can be extracted from it; yet, in general, not much would have been lost had it never been written.

Lerner has shown[2] that Keynes is confused in his terminology (p. 223). There is indeed a so-called *own* rate of interest for each commodity which comes into the picture

[1] See John H. Williams, *Proceedings of the American Economic Review*, May, 1948, p. 287, note 33.

[2] A. P. Lerner, "The Essential Properties of Interest and Money," *Quarterly Journal of Economics*, May, 1952.

when that particular commodity is being loaned. But the *money* rate of interest is the same whether *expressed* in money or in wheat, for example, since the money rate of interest refers to the fee from lending *money*. The wheat rate of interest comes into question only when *wheat* is being loaned, and this wheat loan rate can also be *expressed* either in money or in wheat. Keynes's discussion in Sec. I, Chap. 17, is confused and is of no real importance.

The *own* rate of interest—the house rate, the wheat rate, and the money rate—is in fact the marginal efficiency of a unit whether that unit be a house, a bushel of wheat, or a sum of money. Now it happens that the rate of interest on money *is* the marginal efficiency of money; but this is a special case. The all-embracing term for the so-called own rate of interest is the *marginal efficiency* rate, or the rate of return over cost from investment in an increment of the capital asset in question.

With respect to the "returns on each commodity," as Keynes puts it here (p. 225), three attributes, possessed in different degrees, must be considered. Some assets produce a yield q. Other assets cannot be held without involving a carrying cost c which must be deducted from the yield if there is any. Finally, there is the asset "money," which has no yield and also no carrying cost, but which has an important attribute, namely, liquidity premium l. In the case of houses, the c and l are negligible; with respect to wheat the q and l are negligible; and with respect to money there is no yield, while the carrying cost is negligible. If the prices (in terms of money) of houses and wheat remained stable over time, the marginal efficiency (call it r) of each of the three commodities could be expressed as follows (the subscript 1 applying to houses, 2 to wheat, and 3 to money):

Houses: $r_1 = q_1$
Wheat: $r_2 = -c_2$
Money: $r_3 = l_3$

But cognizance must also be taken of the possible anticipated appreciation a (or depreciation $-a$) of an asset in terms of money. In this event the marginal efficiency of each asset could then be set down as follows (pp. 227–228):

$$\text{Houses:} \quad r_1 = a_1 + q_1$$
$$\text{Wheat:} \quad r_2 = a_2 - c_2$$
$$\text{Money:} \quad r_3 = l_3$$

Now the marginal efficiency of money (*i.e.*, the rate of interest) can rise very high but cannot fall below a certain minimum. On the contrary, in the case of other commodities, the marginal efficiency rate cannot rise very high but can easily fall to zero. The marginal efficiency of money, it must be remembered, is, in fact, the rate of interest. It follows therefore that under certain conditions even though the marginal efficiency of capital assets in general may be moderately high, the rate of interest in a liquidity crisis may rise even higher, thereby choking off further investment, while in other circumstances, even though the rate of interest is at its minimum, the marginal efficiency of capital assets may be falling so low that no investment is possible. Why are these things true?

Money has a low elasticity of production (under gold-standard conditions). Therefore, in view of the inelasticity of supply, a sharp rise in the demand for money may drive the marginal efficiency of money (*i.e.*, the rate of interest) very high (p. 230). But the supply of most capital assets can readily be increased when the demand rises; hence the increase in the r of such assets is checked.

Similarly, most capital assets have a high elasticity of substitution. If the value is rising under the influence of an expanding demand, substitutes flow in and check the rise in the value of the asset in question. But in the case of money the elasticity of substitution is virtually zero. A sharp rise in the demand for money may thus drive its marginal efficiency (*i.e.*, the rate of interest) very high (p. 231).

Finally, there are a number of special reasons why the rate of interest cannot fall indefinitely, even though, via a fall of wages and prices, the money supply should rise *relative* to money income. A fall in money wage rates may produce an expectation of a further fall. This will affect very unfavorably the marginal efficiency of capital assets in general. A fall in wage rates will indeed release cash from the transactions sphere and so tend to reduce the rate of interest. But there are compelling reasons, as we have seen, why the "money-rate of interest will often prove reluctant to decline adequately" (p. 232) even when there is a relative increase in the quantity of money. Moreover, this particular means of reducing the rate of interest is likely to prove ineffective *in practice* in view of the stickiness of money wages (pp. 232–233). Finally, even though the money supply *relative* to income were greatly increased by a fall in money wages, the schedule of liquidity preference may become increasingly elastic at low rates of interest so that "money's yield from liquidity does not fall in response to an increase in its quantity to anything approaching the extent to which the yield from other types of assets falls when their quantity is comparably increased" (p. 233).

Thus "a rise in the money-rate of interest" retards the output of other capital assets where production is elastic, without stimulating the output of money (p. 234). The money rate of interest sets the pace (p. 235) for all the other "commodity rates" (*i.e.*, the marginal efficiency rates for capital assets). Money, with zero or small elasticities of production and substitution (p. 236), is an asset whose marginal efficiency (*i.e.*, liquidity premium or rate of interest) "declines more slowly, as output increases, than the marginal efficiencies of capital assets" (p. 236).

The "expectation that money-wages will be relatively

stable . . . enhances money's liquidity-premium" (p. 238). If wages were fixed (as currently in the United States in certain contracts like that of General Motors) "in terms of wage-goods," *i.e.*, in terms of a price index of consumers' goods, the "effect could only be to cause a violent oscillation of money-prices" (p. 239). It is the stickiness of money wages which prevents small changes in the propensity to consume and the inducement to invest "from producing violent effects on prices" (p. 239). Money would lose the attribute of liquidity if its supply were greatly increased. And its supply, relatively speaking, *would* greatly increase if money wages were highly flexible downward (p. 241).[1]

The peculiarity of money pertains essentially to the characteristic that its liquidity is high relative to its carrying costs (p. 239). In "certain historic environments the possession of land has been characterised by a high liquidity-premium" (p. 241). Moreover "land resembles money in that its elasticities of production and substitution may be very low" (p. 241). The "high rates of interest from mortgages on land, often exceeding the probable net yield from cultivating the land, have been a familiar feature of many agricultural economies" (p. 241). The "competition of a high interest-rate on mortgages may well have had the same effect in retarding the growth of wealth from current investment in newly produced capital-assets, as high interest rates on long-term debts have had in more recent times" (p. 241).

Keynes argued that the world remains poor in capital assets, not because of a high propensity to consume, but because of the high liquidity premiums "formerly attaching to the ownership of land and now attaching to money" (p. 242). This is surely an oversimplification. Liquidity preference may indeed play a role, but equally important is the interest-

[1] "Money itself rapidly loses the attribute of 'liquidity' if its future supply is expected to undergo sharp changes" (footnote, p. 241).

inelasticity of the investment-demand function, by reason of which the marginal efficiency of capital is quickly driven below the minimum rate of interest. Accordingly, before there can be any inducement to add to a stock of capital which is already sufficiently large to provide high living standards, new technological advances must be made. In the final analysis it is technology that determines living standards. The stock of capital which is required for any given level of technology can relatively quickly be provided in advanced communities. In this connection the reader is invited to turn to the illuminating analysis made by John Stuart Mill in Book IV, Chap. IV, of his *Principles*.

There does emerge from Keynes's Chap. 17, as Lerner[1] has pointed out, the highly significant conclusion that money would lose its essential quality, namely, reasonable stability of purchasing power, if money wages lost their stickiness. If money wages were completely flexible downward, the ensuing racing deflation would rob money of its unique attribute. A progressive deflation would drive an economy into barter. The essential attribute of money can be destroyed just as surely by a violent deflation as by an astronomical inflation. This is obviously something which deserves serious consideration if one wishes to appraise the validity of the so-called Pigou effect. Wage stickiness and reasonable price stability are essential if money is to retain its most essential property.

[1] *Op. cit.*, pp. 191–193.

CHAPTER 9

The General Theory of Employment Restated

[GENERAL THEORY, CHAPTER 18]

Keynes begins this chapter by stating what elements in the economic system he regards as given. Changes in these factors may indeed occur, but the effects of such changes are not taken account of in his theoretical system. The most important *given* elements are the quality and quantity of labor and capital equipment, existing technique, degree of competition, consumer tastes, and the social structure which determines the distribution of income.

There remain the independent variables and the dependent variables of his system. The independent variables are the behavior patterns of the society—the basic functions or relationships which underlie Keynes's theory. He does not quite spell them out fully here, but if one takes account of his complete system, it is fair to put them down as follows:

1. The consumption function
2. The marginal efficiency of investment schedule
3. The liquidity preference schedule
4. The quantity of money fixed by the monetary authority

All these variables are stated in terms of the wage unit, which is fixed by bargaining.

Finally there are the dependent variables:

1. The national income, and the volume of employment
2. The rate of interest (p. 245)

Keynes, in fact, makes the rate of interest an independent variable (p. 245). But this is wrong. His mistake follows from the fact that he often, perhaps generally, made the rate of interest depend exclusively on liquidity preference and the quantity of money. Here indeed he makes the rate of interest serve as an independent variable in place of the two underlying functions, liquidity preference and supply of money, which are supposed to fix the rate of interest. In fact, the rate of interest is a determinate, not a determinant. The rate of interest and the national income are together mutually determined by the three basic functions listed above, together with the quantity of money.

Back of the consumption schedule is the psychological propensity to consume; back of the marginal efficiency schedule is the psychological expectation of future yields from capital assets; and back of the liquidity schedule is the psychological attitude to liquidity (expectations with respect to future interest rates). In addition to these independent variables, rooted in behavior patterns and in expectations, there is the quantity of money determined by the action of the Central Bank—an institutional behavior pattern (pp. 246–247).

Thus the *determinants* of the system are (1) the factors which are assumed to be given and (2) the four behavior patterns listed above. The division of the determinants into these two groups—the given factors and the four behavior patterns—is of course more or less arbitrary and is based entirely on experience. The factors which are regarded as given are the factors which are thought to change so slowly that their short-term variation is negligible. It is therefore the changes which occur in the independent variables or behavior patterns which are regarded as *mainly* influencing the system.

Economics is so complex a study that one can hope to find only the *main* determinants of income and employment. This is the theoretical aspect of the problem. Related thereto would be the policy question: What variables are susceptible to social control for the promotion of desirable economic goals (p. 247)?

A brief over-all summary of the determinants of income and employment is presented in Keynes's Sec. II, Chap. 18. Following this concise formulation are two paragraphs which deserve particular attention, for they have generally been overlooked by those critics who have argued that Keynes oversimplified and made his theoretical apparatus too rigid. Here he emphasized the repercussions of the process of income determination upon the position of equilibrium itself. All the determinants, he said, are subject to change, and so the actual course of events is likely to be highly complex. Nevertheless the Keynesian determinants "seem to be the factors which it is useful and convenient to isolate" (p. 249). In the nature of the case no theoretical schema can adequately take account of all the complexity of economic life. Our practical intuition must supplement and correct our theory, for only so can we "take account of a more detailed complex of facts than can be treated on general principles" (p. 249). By isolating the main variables, the material becomes less intractable to work upon and more manageable for reaching a balanced judgment.

Experience teaches us—we could hardly learn this, he says, from logic—that the economic system, though it fluctuates, is not violently unstable. Indeed it seems "capable of remaining in a chronic condition of sub-normal activity for a considerable period without any marked tendency either towards recovery or towards complete collapse" (p. 249). There is no persistent tendency towards a full-employment equilibrium. Sustained cumulative movements up or down are not our normal lot. Upward or downward thrusts quickly wear themselves out and reverse themselves. Price movements, after being initiated by some disturbance (one thinks of the Korean crisis in 1950), "seem to be able to find a level at which they can remain, for the time being, moderately stable" (p. 250)-(Witness the prolonged stability of prices in the United States after February, 1951.)

The "facts of experience do not follow of logical necessity"[1] (p. 250). But they suggest that the system must operate under certain conditions of stability. One such condition would seem to be that the multiplier (based on the marginal propensity to consume) is not very large. Second, such changes in prospective yields or in interest rates as are actually experienced are not "associated with very great changes in the rate of investment" (p. 250). Third, moderate changes in employment "are not associated with very great changes in money-wages," and prices are usually reasonably stable (p. 251). Fourth, whenever the system "overshoots" itself, a reverse movement sets in, in due course. If investment, for example, overshoots its long-run trend, the marginal efficiency of capital is affected unfavorably.

Going back over the ground sketched above point by point, Keynes finds it reasonable to suppose that the multiplier is not very large since as "real income increases, both the pressure of present needs diminishes and the margin over the established standard of life is increased" (p. 251). When income rises, consumption expands, "but by less than the full increment of real income" (p. 251). This "psychological law" Keynes finds to be plausible because our known *experience* would be extremely different "if the law did not hold" (p. 251). For if it did not hold, an increase of investment would set going a cumulative expansion which would go on and on until full employment is reached.

It is of interest to note that J. R. Hicks takes a position precisely the opposite of this in his *Trade Cycle*. Hicks assumes that the multiplier, aided by the accelerator, is sufficiently large so that the economy tends to hit the ceiling of full employment.

---

[1] John Dickinson, a member of the Constitutional Convention of 1787, is said to have appealed to the delegates as follows: "Gentlemen, experience must be our guide; reason may mislead us."

With respect to the second point—moderate fluctuations in investment despite fairly sharp changes in prospective yields—Keynes suggests that an explanation may be found in the supply conditions in the fixed-capital producing industries. A high rate of investment activity will raise the cost of producing capital goods, and this will lower the marginal efficiency of investment.

In regard to the third point—wage movements—experience shows that wage rates are relatively sticky. If this were not so, competition between unemployed workers would lead to violent "instability in the price level" (p. 253). And if money wages were highly flexible upward as well as downward, would not full employment quickly produce violent inflation?

The chapter closes with a brief analysis of the business cycle which, though no reference is cited, runs very much in terms of Aftalion's theory.[1] The econometric model suggested by Keynes involves *self-limiting* factors which cause a reverse movement before full employment is reached; and similarly these same self-limiting factors set a fairly high floor to a depression.[2]

[1] See my *Business Cycles and National Income*, W. W. Norton & Company, 1951, Chap. 18.

[2] See my *Monetary Theory and Fiscal Policy*, McGraw-Hill Book Company, Inc., 1949, pp. 148–150.

Book Five

Money Wages and Prices

CHAPTER 10

The Role of Money Wages

[GENERAL THEORY, CHAPTER 19]

In the chapters we have thus far canvassed, a good deal has been said, here and there, about money wages and about the role of *flexibility* or *stickiness*, as the case may be, of money wages. As the argument has progressed, it has become increasingly necessary to explore this subject more thoroughly than was possible at the beginning, when the fundamental functional relations underlying the Keynesian system had not yet been adequately formulated. This exploration was all the more necessary since classical theory continued (especially under the leadership of Pigou) to assume that wage-rate fluidity provided the economic system with a self-adjustment mechanism that tended always toward full employment. Wage rigidity, it was said, was to blame for any prevailing maladjustment. This Keynes denied, though he was prepared to admit, as we shall see, that a fall in wages and prices, once achieved, might, *under certain conditions*, promote rising employment. Abstracting from all the unfavorable short-run dynamic effects, in pure theory one could argue, he asserted, that a fall in wages and prices has *monetary* consequences similar to an outright increase in the quantity of money.

But first some preliminary considerations. A reduction in money wage rates in any one particular firm or industry will certainly affect employment favorably. This no one can doubt. And the reason is that such a reduction in money wages reduces costs, while on the other side it involves little or no change in the demand for the products of the firm or industry.

173

But what if money wage rates are reduced all round? Will this not affect Aggregate Demand? This is the crucial question. Will Aggregate Demand fall *pari passu* with the decline in money wage rates? And if so, will the effect not be wholly neutral on employment?

Whether Aggregate Demand will fall *proportionately* with any fall in money wage rates depends partly upon what happens to the nonwage groups. The greater the possibility of substituting lower priced labor for other factors of production, the more will wage declines tend to push nonwage money incomes down in line with money wages.[1] If this happens, the effect will be to drive Aggregate Demand down in proportion to the fall in money wages. Assume, however, that nonwage incomes do not decline. Still, if in view of falling prices these groups choose merely to maintain their former consumption standards, then any fall in prices (due to wage declines) will induce a proportional decline in the aggregate money spendings of nonwage earners. In this event both prices and Aggregate Demand will tend to fall proportionately with the decline in money wages.[2]

Wage rates, aggregate outlays, and employment are an interdependent complex which must be viewed as a whole. One cannot assume that aggregate money outlay is independent of the wage rate. A reduction in the wage rate may carry with it, as we have seen, an equiproportionate reduction in money income and total outlay. Pigou[3] has accepted this view, but only in the special case in which the money rate of interest is prevented from falling whenever downward pressure is exerted on it through lower money wage rates. This special case

---

[1] See p. 266, where Keynes refers to "the response of other elements of marginal prime cost to the falling wage-unit."

[2] See Harrod's excellent review of A. C. Pigou's "Theory of Unemployment," *Economic Journal*, March, 1934.

[3] See A. C. Pigou, *Agenda*, August, 1944, and *Lapses from Full Employment*, The Macmillan Company, 1945.

is the so-called Keynesian case, in which the liquidity preference schedule is highly elastic with respect to the rate of interest, so that any release of money from the transaction sphere to the asset sphere is unable to depress appreciably the rate of interest.

Keynes found no simple answer to the problem of wage reduction and its effect on employment. His analysis is pragmatic and leads to an agnostic position. In some circumstances, the effect will be favorable; in others, not. All we can do is to apply our analysis to a variety of assumed conditions.

In Sec. II, Chap. 19, Keynes appraised the problem in terms of his particular method of analyzing income and employment changes. Accordingly, he wished to know whether or not wage reductions will change the propensity to consume, the schedule of the marginal efficiency of capital, and the rate of interest (under which he subsumed, here as elsewhere, the liquidity preference schedule and the quantity of money).

Now these schedules are always subject to shifts due to changes in expectations. What will be the effect of wage reductions on expectations (p. 261)? Entrepreneurs will expect lower costs, and they *may* for the time being discount the fall in Aggregate Demand due to all-round wage cuts. Thus they may expand operations. But will they be able to sell the increased output, or will it merely pile up in the form of increased inventories? Over the long run a larger output and employment can be maintained only if Aggregate Demand has increased, *i.e.*, only if larger investment outlays can be sustained or if the propensity to consume has risen. Larger investment outlays can be maintained only if the marginal efficiency of capital has risen or the rate of interest has fallen. Would wage reductions cause such changes (p. 262)?

1. Wage reductions may have the effect of redistributing income. Wage incomes will fall more than *rentier* incomes. But entrepreneurs will also lose to the *rentier* class. The net effect

is problematical, but on balance income distribution may be more unequal as a result of wage reductions. The transfer from wage earners to other groups is "likely to diminish the propensity to consume" (p. 262). The net result is "more likely to be adverse than favorable" to Aggregate Demand.[1]

2. In an open system, the effect of wage reductions will be favorable for employment since the export position of the wage-cutting countries will become more favorable vis-à-vis other countries, assuming that they do not also cut wages.

3. In an open system, wage cuts (leading to lower export prices) will tend to worsen the terms of trade (p. 263). This may cause a reduction in real income. At a lower real income the *ratio* of consumption to income may indeed rise, but this would not prove, as Keynes has it, that the *propensity* to consume would increase.

4. If a wage cut leads to expectations of *higher* wage rates later on, the net effect on expectations would be favorable. But if it is thought that wage rates will fall still lower, the effect would be unfavorable.

5. Lower wages will reduce the aggregate volume of money transactions and so release money from the transactions sphere to the asset sphere. More money being available for the speculative motive, this means that we would move down on the "pure" liquidity preference schedule L'' and so the rate of interest would tend to fall. A lower rate of interest would be favorable to investment, assuming the investment-demand schedule to be reasonably interest-elastic. But if the wage reductions created political and social unrest, the effect might be to cause unfavorable business expectations, which might cause a downward *shift* of the investment-demand schedule

[1] The unfavorable effect of wage reductions upon income distribution, tending to reduce the propensity to consume, may more than offset any favorable effect from the rise in the real value of money assets—the "Pigou effect."

and an upward *shift* of the pure liquidity preference schedule. Thus, the effect would vary according to circumstances, and so far as pure theory is concerned, we would have to say that no definitive conclusion can be reached.

6. Labor psychology is especially important. Labor troubles may offset otherwise favorable expectations. Each particular group of workers will believe it to their own interest to resist wage reductions. A cut in money wage rates will arouse labor much more than a "gradual and automatic lowering of real wages as a result of rising prices" (p. 264).

7. Any favorable business expectations will be more or less offset by the depressing effect on investment of a greater burden of debt, both public and private.

Leaving aside for the moment the possible (or probable) unfavorable effects of wage reductions on employment, it appeared clear to Keynes that the most hopeful results must be looked for in the possible favorable effects under certain conditions (1) on the marginal efficiency of capital and (2) on the rate of interest.

Assume that wages *have* already been reduced and that no further cuts will be made, so that any expected changes would be upward. This would be the most favorable case. The worst possible case for business expectations would be that of slowly sagging wage rates (p. 265). Taking account of the "actual practices and institutions of the contemporary world" a stable wage policy is likely to have a more favorable effect on business expectations than a flexible policy under which wages would drift downward "by easy stages" as unemployment increased.

Keynes concluded that "those who believe in the self-adjusting quality of the economic system must rest the weight of their argument" on the effect of "a falling wage- and price-level on the demand for money" (p. 266). Theoretically we can "produce precisely the same effects on the rate of interest by reducing wages, whilst leaving the quantity of money unchanged, that we can produce by increasing the quantity of money whilst leaving the level of wages unchanged" (p. 266). But it does not follow that wage reductions can necessarily secure full employment any more than that an increase in the quantity of money can secure full employment. That all depends on the interest-elasticity of the liquidity preference schedule and on the interest-elasticity of the investment-demand schedule. If the former is highly elastic and the latter highly inelastic, increasing the quantity of money will accomplish virtually nothing. A moderate increase in the quantity of money may be inadequate, while an immoderate increase may shatter confidence. The same is true of moderate and immoderate decreases in wage rates (pp. 266–267). Keynes ended this analysis with the assertion that a flexible wage policy is incapable of maintaining continuous full employment. "The economic system cannot be made self-adjusting along these lines" (p. 267).

Yet while wage policy and monetary policy come analytically to very much the same thing, there is a "world of difference between them" (p. 267) in practice.[1] Only a "foolish person" would prefer a "flexible wage policy to a flexible money policy" (p. 268).

The chief result of a flexible wage policy would be "to cause a great instability of prices, so violent perhaps as to make business calculations futile" in a society such as ours. A really flexible wage policy would make a free-price system unworkable. Such a system requires for its proper functioning a reasonably stable value of the monetary unit, and wage stability is basic to monetary stability (pp. 269–271).

A word must be added about the so-called Pigou effect, which Keynes entirely overlooked in his canvass of possible effects of wage reductions on employment. He did consider

[1] These points are elaborated on pp. 267–269 (*General Theory*).

the possibility that wage reductions might change the propensity to consume. For Keynes, however, the shift in the consumption function was thought to come from changes in the distribution of income incident to wage reductions. For Pigou, the shift was thought to come from the increase in the real value of money assets incident to a fall in money wages and prices. Redistribution of income unfavorable to labor would tend to shift the function downward; the rise in real value of money assets would tend to shift it upward.

There is no evidence that Keynes ever thought of the Pigou effect. It had been stated only vaguely in the long controversy (prior to the appearance of the *General Theory*) about the consequences of declining prices. Pigou, in his later work, gives no comprehensive analysis of the various consequences of wage and price reductions but concentrates exclusively on the "real-value-of-money-assets" effect. A more balanced view would seek to assess the *net* effect, taking account of all significant factors. This Keynes sought to do; but he did overlook the Pigou effect. Reference is often made to the "Keynes effect" (falling interest rate due to wage reductions) in contrast to the Pigou effect. But this is singling out only one of the many strands in Keynes's analysis.

In considering wage reductions we may distinguish between (1) the consequences of the *process* of wage reduction, small or large, gradual or rapid, etc. (dynamic analysis); and (2) the effect of a *completed* wage reduction (static analysis). On a different plane one may consider (1) the short-run (or cycle) effects and (2) the long-run (or secular) effects.[1]

[1] It is often said that the Pigou-effect analysis cannot and should not be applied to the problems of the actual world, since the world as we find it does not have the characteristics which are assumed in the rigorous abstractions of the pure theory. But if the analysis stopped there, it would amount merely to an entertaining exercise. We cannot escape from the question: What are the consequences of wage reductions in the world as we find it? It is however true that it is not useful to consider short-run price and wage

Take the *cycle* effects viewed in terms of the static analysis. Reduction of wage costs *having been completed*, will the larger real value of money assets raise the consumption function so that full employment can be assured, assuming that other expansionist factors are weak? The answer appears to be in the negative, since as recovery progresses, prices will begin to rise and so the real value of money assets will progressively fall. Instead of a reinforcing factor, the "real-asset effect," which is supposed to drive the economy on to full employment, begins to vanish once the lower turning point in the cycle is reached. Note that the analysis here made runs strictly in terms of static analysis (a high level of abstraction) and not in terms of the dynamic effects of short-run expectations. It applies to a situation like that of 1936 to 1940 in the United States, when prices *had* fallen and become stabilized *at a lower level*.

If one considers the problem from the *long-run* angle, the Pigou effect would presumably act to cushion, a little, each succeeding depression. Thus each succeeding cycle, it could be argued, would have a higher bottom. But this does not appear to be very convincing as a positive force to achieve full employment.

The Pigou-effect analysis should be integrated with the old problem of the relative merits of stable prices vs. a long-run downward trend in prices, for that is what it essentially comes to. The real value of money assets will rise if the long-run trend of prices is downward. This could be achieved either in a mild form (in a society enjoying advances in man-hour

---

movements, since in this case the unfavorable dynamic effects predominate. The static relations considered by Pigou are, however, not seriously violated in the case of long-run or secular price and wage movements. This is true because, with respect to slow-moving secular trends, the important consideration is not the rate of change but rather the fact that prices have settled at a lower level.

productivity) by holding money wages constant or in more drastic form by wage reductions. Under the long-run downward trend of prices, the real value of money assets would steadily grow, and so the Pigou effect would gradually take hold. The *rentier* class would indeed experience a rise in the real value of their money assets, but entrepreneurs would be adversely affected, and it is hard to believe that on balance the mass of consumers would find themselves "richer" after thirty or forty years of falling prices. And this is at least partly due to the fact that their employment position might well be worsened by the unfavorable effect of a secular downward trend in prices on business profits compared with the condition of a stable (or perhaps even slowly advancing) price level. It is probably a fair statement to say that economists are largely in agreement that, for this and other reasons, a stable price level is to be preferred to a long-run downward trend in prices.

Finally, the Pigou-effect analysis assumes too readily that we have definite knowledge about how an increase in the real value of money assets affects the propensity to save. We in fact know very little about it. Against the easy assumption usually made, we can advance the familiar saying, at least equally plausible, that a little nest egg of savings whets the appetite for more. This bit of folklore is reinforced by the findings of the Consumer Survey Institute,[1] that only a comparatively small proportion of *each* of the lower income groups holds any appreciable amount of assets. The individuals who save seem to be rather rare birds, just the kind of people whose appetite for saving would grow as their stock pile of liquid assets increased. And lastly, the Pigou effect must be weighed quantitatively. We need to know how the money assets are distributed, and whether the amount held by the mass of con-

[1] See "Survey of Consumer Finances," published periodically in the *Federal Reserve Bulletin*.

sumers, say 80 per cent, is of a magnitude sufficient to have much effect, granted that the tendency really works in the direction usually assumed. Even as a matter of pure theory, it is not enough to disclose a tendency; it is also necessary to assess the strength or weakness of the tendency.[1]

On balance it must be said that Keynes's analysis of the effects of wage reductions is pretty comprehensive and illuminating. It is indeed not complete. But it has many facets. It is not limited to the interest-rate effect, which is often singled out as the Keynes effect.

The so-called Keynes effect and the Pigou effect both reflect *monetary* consequences of wage reductions. In both cases, the effect envisaged could be achieved far more effectively, not by wage reductions, but by a deliberate expansion of money-asset holdings through a government deficit financed by the Central Bank. In the case of a deliberate expansion of money assets, the unfavorable effects of *lower* prices (on profits) and of *falling* prices would be avoided while the favorable effects would be more pronounced. Moreover, it is one thing to assume that full employment can be assured by an *automatic* adjustment process (as Pigou does) and quite a different thing to propose, as Keynes did, a positive monetary and fiscal program of expansion.

[1] In periods of depression and unemployment (and also when goods are scarce, as in war devastated countries), the widespread holdings of monetary assets certainly have expansionist (and inflationary) effects.

CHAPTER 11

The Keynesian Theory of Money and Prices

[GENERAL THEORY, CHAPTERS 20, 21]

Chapters 20 and 21 can best be considered together. They deal with the same subject matter, namely, the complexity of the relationship between changes in Aggregate Demand and changes in the price level, or more broadly the relationship between changes in the quantity of money and changes in prices. In these two chapters Keynes applied to the theory of money and prices the tools of analysis which he had developed earlier. Moreover, his own analysis is compared with the Quantity Theory.

The Keynesian analysis runs in terms of supply and demand functions; and it takes cognizance of the changing elasticities of these functions at different points in the schedules. The manner in which changes in the quantity of money exert their effect on prices is traced through a complicated set of inter-relationships. The degree of influence depends upon the elasticities of the functions at every point.

The effect of changes in the quantity of money on prices is not direct and proportional, as the older Quantity Theory had it. Instead, there is "many a slip, twixt the cup and the lip." First there is the relation between money and Aggregate Demand. Then there is the effect of changes in Aggregate Demand on output on the one side and on prices on the other. Here we encounter elasticities of supply price at different output levels. But this is not all. Account must also be taken of changes in

183

wage rates, whether induced by changes in Demand or autonomously determined by trade-union action and collective bargaining.

Keynes's theory concentrates attention upon the *behavior of the community*, which behavior is analyzed in terms of the Keynesian functions and the various elasticities discussed in these chapters. In contrast, the Quantity Theory concentrates attention upon the behavior of the Central Bank, which behavior expresses itself in the quantity of money.

Chapter 21 begins with a complaint that economics has been divided into two compartments with no doors or windows between the *theory of value* and the *theory of money and prices*. In the case of value theory, the traditional analysis deals with the elasticities of Supply and Demand. But in the theory of money, the elasticity of Supply has in the simpler Quantity Theory discussions become zero, and Demand has been thought to be proportional to the quantity of money. Keynes, however, wished to introduce the concept of elasticity no less into the theory of money than in the theory of value. Accordingly, he is concerned with (1) the elasticities of prices in response to changes in Aggregate Demand and (2) the elasticity of Aggregate Demand in response to changes in the quantity of money. The theory of money and the theory of value would thus become integrated into one theory.

Economics might perhaps usefully be divided between the theory of the individual industry or firm and the theory of output and employment as a whole. Still more significant, he suggests, would be a division between (1) the theory of stationary (static) equilibrium and (2) the theory of shifting equilibrium. The latter involves changing views about the future which influence the present situation. Here money enters, for it is the all important *"link between the present and the future"* (p. 293).

The theory of shifting equilibrium involves the "problems of the real world in which our previous expectations are liable to disappointment" and in which "expectations concerning the future affect what we do today" (pp. 293–294). Here the "peculiar properties of money as a link between the present and the future must enter into our calculations" (p. 294). The theory of shifting equilibrium, while it must be pursued in terms of money, still "remains a theory of value and distribution" and not merely a theory of money (p. 294). We cannot "even begin to discuss the effect of changing expectations on current activities except in monetary terms" (p. 294).

The general price level depends upon (1) wage rates, to which must be added the rates of remuneration of other factors which enter into marginal cost, and (2) the scale of output as a whole. Since wage rates are by far the most important part of total factor costs, and since the remuneration of the other factors tends to change in more or less the same proportion as wage rates, we may say that the general price level is basically (in the short run where equipment and technique are taken as given) a function of (1) the level of wage rates and (2) the scale of output (pp. 294–295). Changes in the quantity of money operate (if at all) on prices through the effect of such changes on wage rates and on output. A more complete statement would be that changes in the quantity of money may affect Aggregate Demand; and changes in Aggregate Demand will affect wage rates and output according to the prevailing elasticities of wage rates and of output with respect to changes in Demand. Thus changes in the price level can in the first instance be explained in terms of changes in wage rates (or, more comprehensively, *factor cost*) and of changes in the scale of output; but these in turn are affected by changes in Demand.

QUANTITY THEORY VS. KEYNESIAN THEORY

As a preliminary step toward an examination of the complexities of the real world, Keynes suggested some simplifying assumptions in part in accordance with the Quantity Theory tradition. Assume that the supply curve is perfectly elastic so long as there is any unemployment. This implies that workers are content with the same money wage so long as there is any unemployment and also that nonwage factors are available in ample supply at constant rates of remuneration [or else that "all unemployed resources are homogeneous and interchangeable" (p. 295)]. Under these assumptions output will change in the same proportion as Aggregate Demand, which is here assumed to change in the same proportion as the quantity of money. If now the supply curve becomes perfectly *inelastic* as soon as full employment is reached, then "*prices* will change in the same proportion as the quantity of money" (p. 296). This is the Quantity Theory of money.

But the real world is more complicated than these assumptions would have it. Effective Demand will not change in proportion to changes in the quantity of money; prices will not change in proportion to changes in Aggregate Demand; marginal cost will rise as employment increases[1] (certainly true of agriculture and, Keynes thought, also of industry); bottlenecks will arise before full employment is reached; money wage rates will tend to rise before full employment is reached; and finally the remuneration of factors other than labor will not change in the same proportion as money wage rates. Taking account of all these complications, it is evident that the simplified Quantity Theory does not hold.

An increase in Effective Demand will partly spend itself in

---

[1] Output rises proportionally less than employment, owing to diminishing returns. At this point in the analysis changes in O and N are not assumed to be proportional.

an increase in output and partly in an increase in prices. The theory of money and prices must first answer the question, how Effective Demand responds to changes in the quantity of money and second, how the effects of changes in Aggregate Demand are divided between changes in output and changes in prices.

Keynes had something here to say about the nature of economic thinking. Economic tools of analysis do not "provide a machine, or method of blind manipulation, which will furnish an infallible answer" (p. 297). The great fault of symbolic or mathematical methods of "formalising a system of economic analysis" is that they "expressly assume strict independence between the factors involved" (p. 297). In "ordinary discourse" we can take account of the necessary reservations, qualifications, and adjustments. Too often mathematical economics rests on "initial assumptions" which do not take adequate cognizance of the "complexities and interdependencies of the real world" (pp. 297–298).

In Sec. IV, Chap. 21, the complexities encountered in a realistic theory of money and prices are considered in some detail. Keynes warns the reader that also his own analysis presents a deceptive simplicity. In so far as changes in the quantity of money affect prices, Keynes's analysis seeks to discover the connection primarily via the influence of such changes on the rate of interest. Stated in a broader way, the effect could conveniently be derived from the liquidity preference schedule, the investment-demand schedule, and the propensity-to-consume schedule (which gives us the investment multiplier). But this analysis (i.e., the Keynesian analysis), though valuable, still falls short of the goal, says Keynes, because these functions are themselves partly dependent upon the elasticities of output and of factor costs (i.e., money wage rates and the remuneration of other factors) with respect to changes in Aggregate Demand. This is true, for example, of the marginal efficiency of capital (investment-demand schedule), which is determined in part by the cost of capital goods, and such cost will depend to a degree upon the elasticity of supply. Moreover, monetary policy may change expectations with respect to the investment outlook. Similar illustrations can be cited to show how the liquidity preference schedule and the consumption function may be shifted up or down by various complicating factors. Taking account of all these functions and the influences exerted upon them by a variety of shifting circumstances there will indeed be a determinate increase in Effective Demand corresponding to, and in equilibrium with, a given increase in the quantity of money (p. 299). But the interrelation is highly complex, and the analysis involved is very far from being the Quantity Theory of money.

The "income-velocity-of-money" approach, Keynes thinks, explains nothing. Income velocity depends on "many complex and variable factors" (p. 299). This approach obscures, as Keynes sees it, the "real character of the causation." What needs to be explained is fluctuations in Effective Demand, and this cannot be done by means of a mechanical ratio of realized income to money supply. Causation must be found in terms of expectations and the behavior patterns (the basic Keynesian functions) upon which changes in expectations operate. Effective Demand "corresponds to the income, the expectation of which has set production moving" (p. 299).

So much for a preliminary statement. But now we must come to grips with the more detailed analysis. Keynes might, indeed, have improved his exposition if he had combined Chaps. 20 and 21 into one. Chapter 20 purports to deal with the relation of *employment* to Effective Demand. In fact, however, the chapter quickly swings into a discussion of the response of *output* to changes in Aggregate Demand. To be sure, Keynes often assumed (though he departs from this assumption when he introduces diminishing returns from labor) that changes in output are, in the short run, associated with corresponding changes in employment.

Chapter 20 begins, however, with the employment function, the relation of employment to Effective Demand. The employment function for the economy as a whole (p. 282) may be written $N = F(D_w)$.† Here Demand is measured in terms of wage rates so that any dissipation of Effective Demand (in *money* terms) caused by an increase in money wage rates is ruled out. The effect of increases in money wage rates is considered later in connection with the relationship of changes in Aggregate Demand to changes in the price level.

Keynes's employment function $N = F(D_w)$ may usefully be compared with Pigou's equation $N = \dfrac{qY}{W}$, in which N is employment, q is that fraction of money income which is paid to workers, Y is money income, and W is the money wage rate. Pigou's equation stresses the point that changes in money income, which are offset by corresponding changes in wage rates, will leave employment unchanged. Similarly, Keynes makes employment a function of Demand corrected for wage changes.

$N = F(D_w)$ is the employment function for industry as a whole (p. 282). But in order to know the demand function for each separate industry, it is necessary to know the input-output relations (Leontief) of various interrelated industries in the whole economy. For any given level of Effective Demand in terms of wage units, D_w, there will be an array of employment functions F_r for each individual industry; and the sum of these separate employment functions will equal the aggregate employment function. Thus $\Sigma F_r(D_w) = F(D_w)$; and $N = \Sigma N_r$, in which N_r‡ represents employment in an individual industry.

† D_w means Aggregate Demand in terms of wage units (*i.e.*, wage rates).

‡ The r subscript in F_r and N_r denotes the function and the employment *in an individual industry.*

The elasticity formulas given on pages 282 to 283 state the rate at which employment (or output as the case may be) will increase when Effective Demand, corrected for wage changes, increases. The elasticity of aggregate employment with respect to Aggregate Demand may be expressed as $\dfrac{dN}{dD_w} \cdot \dfrac{D_w}{N}$. †

If output can be increased scarcely at all as Demand rises (*i.e.*, the elasticity approaches zero), then marginal cost and price would rise sharply in terms of wage rates with each increase in D_w. Price would accordingly rise far above average unit cost, and profits would increase rapidly (p. 283). On the other hand, if the elasticity of output approaches unity, marginal cost (and so unit price) would not rise significantly in relation to wage rates. Accordingly, the margin between price and unit cost would remain constant, and profits per unit of output would not rise (p. 283). Increased Demand would in this case lead to increased real income for all the factors of production.

The latter case could not occur, however, if industry is operating under increasing cost. Keynes, believing that the marginal-cost curve was U-shaped (rather than flat or declining up to the point of full utilization of capacity), assumed that industry does in fact operate in the short run under conditions of increasing marginal cost. He assumed therefore that prices in relation to wage rates must rise as employment expands. This means that real wages must fall. But according to classical theory "real wages are always equal to the marginal dis-

---

† Assume that we start with an average relation of fifty units of D_w to ten units of N but that marginally one additional unit of employment, dN, requires an increment of $10D_w$. Substituting these figures for $\dfrac{DN}{dD_w} \cdot \dfrac{D_w}{N}$, we find that the elasticity of employment with respect to Demand will be $\frac{1}{10} \cdot {}^5\!\%_{10} = \frac{1}{2}$.

utility of labour," and therefore "the labour supply will fall off, *cet. par.*, if real wages are reduced." Accordingly, on classical lines, it is not possible to increase employment by increasing Aggregate Demand. But if in fact unemployed workers are prepared to take jobs at the going rate of money wages, then it is possible to increase employment "by increasing expenditure in terms of money" (p. 284). "The extent to which prices (in terms of wage-units) will rise, *i.e.*, the extent to which real wages will fall, when money expenditure is increased, depends, therefore, on the elasticity of output . . . " (p. 284).

If output elasticity is low, the price elasticity will be high. The sum of the two elasticities is equal to unity. "Effective demand spends itself, partly in affecting output and partly in affecting price, according to this law" (p. 285).

But now assume that values are measured in money, not in wage units. We then get the elasticity of money prices and money wages in response to changes in Effective Demand measured in terms of money. Then the elasticity of price will depend upon the elasticities of output *and* of wage rates. Now since the Quantity Theory held that wages stand in a certain relation to money, this begins to look like the Quantity Theory of money (p. 285). Thus if the elasticity of output is zero and the elasticity of wages is 1, prices will rise in the same proportion as Effective Demand in terms of money (p. 286).

But Effective Demand in each industry will not change in direct proportion to changes in Aggregate Demand. Moreover, the elasticities of output will vary in different industries. Thus relative prices will change when there is a change in the general level of prices (p. 286). Moreover, if Demand is directed to industries with a high elasticity of output and employment, a given increase in Aggregate Demand will cause a large increase in employment. And for the same reason, a change in the direction of Demand may change the volume of employment even though there is no change in Aggregate Demand (p. 286).

Some of these reflections appear somewhat commonplace. But they are worth commenting on here, since it is often said that Keynes always deals in aggregates and takes no cognizance of the condition in different industries. This chapter (among others) shows that this is not always the case. Keynes here stresses the point that employment is not *simply* a function of changes in Aggregate Demand.

This is especially true in the short run in industries in which it is not possible quickly to increase Supply, though given time it may be possible to do so. In this case the elasticity of employment may be low in the short run but nearly unity in the long run (p. 287). Much depends upon the existence of surplus stocks and surplus capacity (p. 288).

When no surplus of labor is available, any further increase of expenditure will cause prices, wages, and profits to rise. Output will not alter, and prices will rise "in exact proportion to MV," that is, to changes in Aggregate Demand (p. 289). There is thus an "asymmetry between Inflation and Deflation" (p. 291). Deflation drives both employment and prices down; inflation can raise only prices, not employment (p. 291).

In general it was Keynes's conclusion that "supply price will increase as output from a given equipment is increased" (p. 300). This would be true, even though there is no change in money wage rates, under conditions of increasing marginal cost. Now there can be no doubt that this is indeed the case with respect to agricultural products, but for industry in general the marginal-cost curve may be flat or even declining up to (or close to) full employment.[1] The situation will, of

---

[1] Keynes was never prepared to accept the view that the marginal-cost curve may be flat. See the elaboration of this matter in my *Monetary Theory and Fiscal Policy*, McGraw-Hill Book Company, Inc., 1949, pp. 107–110.

course, vary with different industries. Keynes thought, indeed, that the supply of some commodities would become "perfectly inelastic" even in conditions of a "substantial surplus of resources" (p. 300). He believed that a series of bottlenecks would be encountered as Demand increases and, for these commodities, prices would rise sharply before full employment was reached.

But the "general level of prices will not rise very much as output increases" so long as there are unemployed resources (p. 300). A *sudden* large increase in Demand will indeed encounter bottlenecks, even though there is widespread unemployment. But if the increased Demand prevails over a longer period, these bottlenecks can often be wholly or substantially broken.

Money wage rates (wage units) tend to rise before full employment is reached owing to pressure from labor groups whenever profits rise. Such wage-rate changes are liable to be discontinuous—a succession of "semi-critical points" (p. 301). To the extent that this occurs the increase in Aggregate Demand is unnecessarily dissipated on higher prices with correspondingly less effect on output and employment. In so far as marginal cost rises as output increases, some part of the increase in Demand *must* be dissipated in higher prices. But if in addition money wage rates also rise, employment suffers as a result of the higher wages of the already employed workers.

ESCALATOR CLAUSES IN WAGE CONTRACTS

The Keynesian analysis of wages and prices throws light upon the policy of tying wage rates to the cost-of-living index —the so-called escalator contracts. It has been suggested that such contracts if applied universally might render completely ineffective the Keynesian policy of increasing employment by manipulating Aggregate Demand. The argument is that under such wage contracts the whole increase in Aggregate Demand will spill over into price and wage increases, leaving no effect whatever on employment. But this is only a half truth, since the price-wage spiral cannot operate in this strictly *proportional* manner unless every increase in Aggregate Demand raised prices by the same percentage rate. If indeed this happened, then wages under the escalator clause would automatically rise along with prices and the spiral would be started. But if there is serious unemployment, prices in fact will rise relatively little at first and therefore the main effect from an increase in Aggregate Demand would be an increase in employment. Prices will not rise much primarily because in manufacturing industry the marginal-cost curve remains relatively flat up to the point at which capacity is pretty fully utilized,[1] and partly because of time lags. Food prices do rise sharply when Aggregate Demand increases, owing to the condition of inelastic supply with respect to agriculture produce.

Accordingly, in view of the rise in food prices, escalator clauses in labor contracts would indeed have the effect of dissipating *some considerable part* of the increase in Aggregate Demand in higher prices. Thus to a degree such clauses do have the effect of reducing the employment-creating power of an increase in Aggregate Demand.

In the absence of escalator clauses, Keynes thought that money wage rates, on balance, would rise relatively little until full employment was approached, and he was therefore hopeful that by far the major effect of an increase in Aggregate Demand would be to raise the level of employment, with relatively little effect on prices.

---

[1] Keynes, to be sure, believed that the marginal-cost curve would begin to rise whenever Aggregate Demand increases, even if the upward movement starts from low employment levels. Keynes therefore would regard cost-of-living escalator clauses as more dangerous than in fact they are.

As full employment is approached, the effect is more and more to increase prices and less and less to increase employment. At this point escalator clauses become dangerously inflationary.

Escalator clauses, as applied in most countries, operate with less inflationary effectiveness than the strict application of the price-wage-spiral principle would indicate.[1] This is true, as we have noted above, partly because of the relative flatness of the marginal-cost curve and partly because there are in fact important time lags between increases in Effective Demand and increases in the price level. And there are further time lags between price increases and the *application* of the scheduled wage increases. Moreover, the escalator clauses apply as yet only to a fraction of the entire economy. In addition, increases in productivity are continually going on, and these tend, unless offset by corresponding wage increases, to lower unit cost. But some collective-bargaining contracts also contain "productivity" clauses which provide for automatic wage increases corresponding to actual or presumed productivity increases.[2]

Productivity clauses taken by themselves alone cannot be said to be inflationary since they would tend to hold unit costs stable. But when they are combined with the cost-of-living escalator, the effect is to minimize the time lags involved in the adjustment of wages to increases in productivity. Thus the combined effect is to enhance the inflationary consequences

[1] Cf. Vera Lutž, "Real and Monetary Factors in the Determination of Employment Levels," *Quarterly Journal of Economics*, May, 1952.

[2] Such productivity clauses may be of two types: (1) workers in each industry would get increases proportional to productivity increases *in their own industry*, and (2) workers in industries would get wage increases proportional to the general over-all increase in productivity in the economy as a whole.

The General Motors contract is of the latter type and is based in a general way on past trends in over-all increases in productivity.

of escalator clauses. Aggregate Demand is thus allowed in part to run to waste in increased prices, and the employment effect is minimized.

The price-wage spiral might, of course, be held in restraint by rigorous controls—rationing and price control. In this event, prices not having risen, the escalator mechanism would not operate. If controls are effective, spiral inflation could indeed be avoided, despite the escalator clauses, but only at the cost of abandoning the free-price-making mechanism. Keynesian employment policy per se does not include such procedures as price controls in normal peacetime conditions. To the extent that escalator clauses reduce the effectiveness, under a free-price system, of an expansionist program, there is accordingly a serious conflict between the Keynesian employment policy and the policy of cost-of-living escalator wage contracts.

But now to return to the main argument.

Keynes admits that it is an oversimplification to assume that the money wage rate (wage unit) adequately represents the "weighted average of the rewards of the factors entering into marginal prime-cost" (p. 302). Still the wage rate is the basic component of the "weighted average of rewards," and so we are not too far off when we say that the money wage rate is "the essential standard of value" (p. 302). The price level depends partly on the wage rate and partly on the scale of output. Thus once again, as in earlier chapters, Keynes emphasizes the point that "we must have *some* factor, the value of which in terms of money is, if not fixed, at least sticky, to give us any stability of values in a monetary system" (p. 304). Essentially it is stability of money wage rates, according to Keynes, that gives stability to the value of money (*i.e.*, the price level). This conclusion is diametrically opposite to that reached by the Quantity Theory.

ELASTICITIES OF THE RELEVANT FUNCTIONS

Let e_p stand for price elasticity with respect to Demand, $\frac{D}{p}\frac{dp}{dD}$;[†] and let e_o mean output elasticity and e_w wage-rate elasticity with respect to Demand. If an increase in Demand has no effect on output while wages rise proportionally, then output elasticity e_o is zero and wage elasticity e_w is 1. Since the elasticity of output is zero, prices (along with wages) will rise in direct proportion to changes in Demand, that is, e_p is unity.

But now we need to introduce (in order to come to grips with the Quantity Theory) one more elasticity—the elasticity of Effective Demand with respect to changes in the quantity of money, that is, e_d. If then we know e_p and e_d, we can easily obtain e, the elasticity of price in response to changes in the quantity of money. For example, if the elasticity of price with respect to Demand, e_p, is ½, and the elasticity of Demand with respect to the quantity of money, e_d, is ½, then the elasticity of price with respect to the quantity of money (namely, e) is ¼. In short, $e = e_p \cdot e_d$.

The elasticity of Demand with respect to changes in the quantity of money $\left(e_d = \frac{M}{D}\frac{dD}{dM}\right)$ represents a very complex relationship involving the liquidity preference schedule in conjunction with the investment-demand schedule, and perhaps also the elasticity of consumption with respect to (1) the rate of interest and (2) changes in the real value of money

† If $\frac{dp}{dD} = \frac{p}{D}$, then the elasticity of Demand with respect to price will be unity, or, in other words, changes in price will be proportional to changes in Demand. Let $dp = 1$ and $dD = 2$; and let $p = 30$ and $D = 60$. Then

$$\frac{dp}{dD} \cdot \frac{D}{p} = \frac{1}{2} \cdot \frac{60}{30} = \frac{1}{1}.$$

assets. Depending upon the slope of the liquidity preference curve, changes in the quantity of money may cause changes in the rate of interest; and changes in the rate of interest in turn (depending upon the slope of the investment-demand schedule) may cause changes in the volume of investment, while consumption may also respond to monetary influences as indicated above. Thus e_d stands for all the Keynesian relationships, and not merely [as Keynes has it (p. 305)] for "the liquidity factors." These are the relations, or behavior patterns, which we must study, if we wish to know how changes in the quantity of money affect Aggregate Demand.

But this is only the first complicated step toward a theory of money and prices. The second step (after discovering how changes in the quantity of money affect Aggregate Demand) has to do with the effect of changes in Aggregate Demand upon the general price level. The price elasticity e_p $\left(\text{that is, } \dfrac{D \, dp}{p \, dD}\right)$ is compounded of two underlying elasticities, namely, $e_o \left(\text{that is, } \dfrac{D \, dO}{O \, dD}\right)$ and $e_w \left(\text{that is, } \dfrac{D \, dW}{W \, dD}\right).$ If we assume $e_w = $ zero, then e_p is simply the complement of e_o since $e_p + e_o = 1.$ This means that any increase in Aggregate Demand D will exhaust itself either in larger output or in higher prices.

If $e_o = 0,$ then the full impact of rising Demand will express itself in a proportionate rise in prices. But if $e_o = 1,$ then prices will not rise at all. Here we are dealing with the "physical factors which determine the rate of increasing returns" (pp. 305–306)—i.e., we are concerned with the marginal-cost curve as affected by diminishing returns, and not with the effect of increasing money wage rates on marginal money cost. If we assume, however, that e_w is greater than zero, i.e., that wages rise more or less in response to an increase in Aggregate Demand, then e_p will rise, not merely because marginal cost rises owing to diminishing returns, but also because of the upward shift in the marginal-cost curve due to the increase in money wage rates. Thus the rise in prices will be greater, for any given increase in output, than would be the case if money wage rates were constant.[1] In this case any given increase in Aggregate Demand will spend itself relatively more in price increases and relatively less in output increases. $e_p + e_o$ will still be equal to 1, but the upward thrust of money wage rates will make e_p larger and e_o smaller.

If $e_d = 1$, then the Marshallian k would be constant and Aggregate Demand (or income) would change in proportion to changes in the quantity of money. If Demand changes in proportion to changes in the money supply, and if the whole increase in Aggregate Demand is swallowed up in increases in money wages ($e_d = 1$, and $e_w = 1$), then prices will change proportionally in response to changes in the quantity of money (that is, $e = 1$), as the Quantity Theory has it. But in the usual case e will be less than unity. In the case of a "flight from the currency," however, the elasticities both of Aggregate Demand and of money wages in response to changes in the quantity of money may become very large, and so the elasticity of the price level with respect to the quantity of money may well in those circumstances be more than unity (p. 306) as illustrated in a number of historical cases following the First World War.

Short-run and Long-run Considerations[2]

Keynes emphasizes (p. 306) the point that the complex relationships which he elaborates in Chap. 21 involve prima-

---

[1] In other words, if money wage rates rise, then output would rise less in response to a given increase in Aggregate Demand than would be the case if wage rates remained constant.

[2] This section is reprinted from my *Monetary Theory and Fiscal Policy, op. cit.*, pp. 139–142.

rily considerations of the short-run effect of changes in the quantity of money on prices. From the long-run standpoint he suggests that some simpler relationship may perhaps be found.

But he thinks that this is a question for historical generalization rather than for pure theory. He suggests that over the long run there may well be some sort of rough relationship between the national income and the quantity of money. Over and above the quantity of money required in the active circulation, he suggests that there may be "some fairly stable proportion of the national income more than which people will not readily keep in the shape of idle balances for long periods together, provided the rate of interest exceeds a certain psychological minimum" (p. 306). Fluctuations in the quantity of "surplus money" (*i.e.*, money in excess of the requirements of the active circulation) will tend to raise and lower the rate of interest (possibly down to the minimum), and such fluctuations in the rate of interest will tend to influence the volume of Effective Demand. "Thus the net effect of fluctuations over a period of time will be to establish a mean figure in conformity with the stable proportion between the national income and the quantity of money to which the psychology of the public tends sooner or later to revert" (p. 307).

The ratio of money to national income in the United States has risen, but at a varying rate of increase, throughout the last 150 years. The money supply was (in round numbers) about 5 per cent of national income in 1800, 15 per cent in 1850, 50 per cent in 1900, and 80 per cent in 1947. In view of the unreliability of early income data these figures are only rough indicators of the trend. Correcting for the secular trend in the ratios here indicated, one could possibly speak of a "stable proportion between the national income and the quantity of money," but this is probably not what Keynes intended to say. If, however, by "stable proportion" one merely means that the ratio of income to money does not simply behave capriciously and in a wholly random fashion, then we are thrown back again to a consideration of the behavior pattern of the community with respect to the quantity of money and its influence on Effective Demand and all the other relationships which we have been analyzing in this chapter.

Keynes believed that the long-run fluctuations and tendencies referred to above would probably work with less friction in the upward than in the downward direction.

[If the] quantity of money remains very deficient for a long time, the escape will be normally found in changing the monetary standard or the monetary system so as to raise the quantity of money, rather than in forcing down the wage-unit and thereby increasing the burden of debt. Thus the very long-run course of prices has almost always been upward. For when money is relatively abundant, the wage-unit rises; and when money is relatively scarce, some means is found to increase the effective quantity of money.

During the nineteenth century, the growth of population and of invention, the opening-up of new lands, the state of confidence and the frequency of war over the average of (say) each decade seem to have been sufficient, taken in conjunction with the propensity to consume, to establish a schedule of the marginal efficiency of capital, which allowed a reasonably satisfactory average level of employment to be compatible with a rate of interest high enough to be psychologically acceptable to wealth owners (p. 307).

The monetary system, particularly the development of bank money, was adjusted so as to ensure a quantity of money sufficient to satisfy the normal liquidity preference at rates of interest seldom much below the gilt-edged rate of 3 or $3\frac{1}{2}$ per cent. Wage rates tended steadily upward, but were largely balanced by increases in efficiency so as to allow a fair measure of stability of prices. This was not an accident. It was due to a "balance of forces in an age when individual groups of employers were strong enough to prevent the wage-unit from rising much faster than the efficiency of production, and when monetary systems were at the same time sufficiently fluid and sufficiently conservative" to provide on balance a quantity of money adequate to establish the lowest rate of interest acceptable by wealth owners in view of their liquidity preferences. "The average level of employment was, of course, substantially below full employment, but not so intolerably below it as to provoke revolutionary changes" (p. 308).

The contemporary problem arises out of the "possibility that the average rate of interest which will allow a reasonable average level of employment is one so unacceptable to wealth owners that it cannot be readily established merely by manipulating the quantity of money (pp. 308–309).

The nineteenth century could find its way because, under the conditions stated above, it could achieve a tolerable level of employment merely by assuring an adequate supply of money in relation to the level of wages. "If this was our only problem now . . . we, today, would certainly find a way" (p. 309).

"But the most stable, and the least easily shifted, element in our contemporary economy has been hitherto, and may prove to be in the future, the minimum rate of interest acceptable to the generality of wealth-owners. If a tolerable level of employment requires a rate of interest much below the average rates which ruled in the nineteenth century, it is most doubtful whether it can be achieved merely by manipulating the quantity of money (p. 309).

From the prospective rate of return on new investment has to be deducted (1) an allowance for risk and uncertainty, (2) the cost of bringing borrowers and lenders together, and (3) income taxes, before we arrive at the *net* return required to tempt the wealth owner to sacrifice his liquidity. "If, in conditions of tolerable average employment, this net yield turns out to be infinitesimal, time-honored methods may prove unavailing (p. 309).

Thus it is that modern countries place primary emphasis on fiscal policy in whose service monetary policy is relegated to the subsidiary role of a useful but necessary handmaiden.

APPENDIX

The following equations, definitions, and brief explanation may help the student to identify easily and quickly the various elasticities discussed in Sec. VI, Chap. 21 (*General Theory*):

$e_p = \dfrac{D}{p}\dfrac{dp}{dD}.$ This means the elasticity of the price level in response to changes in Demand, or, in other words, the extent to which the price level changes as Demand increases. Assume that each increment of Demand (that is, dD) causes a change in the price level of dp. If the relation of dp to the prevailing price level p is proportionate to the relation of dD to D, then the elasticity of the price level with respect to Demand will be unity. Thus if $D = 30$ and $p = 10$, while $\dfrac{dp}{dD} = \dfrac{1}{3}$,

then $\dfrac{D}{p}\dfrac{dp}{dD} = \dfrac{30}{10} \cdot \dfrac{1}{3} = \dfrac{1}{1}.$

The relationship between the two variables might be linear, in which case the elasticity is constant at all levels of Aggregate Demand. More likely the elasticity will be a changing one.

$e_o = \dfrac{D}{O}\dfrac{dO}{dD}.$ This means the elasticity of output O in response to changes in Aggregate Demand D.

$e_w = \dfrac{D}{w}\dfrac{dw}{dD}.$ This represents the elasticity of money wage rates with respect to changes in Aggregate Demand.

$e_d = \dfrac{M}{D}\dfrac{dD}{dM}.$ This stands for the elasticity of Aggregate Demand D with respect to changes in the quantity of money M.

$e = \dfrac{M}{p}\dfrac{dp}{dM}.$ This means the elasticity of price (*i.e.*, the price level) with respect to changes in the quantity of money. It bridges the gap between (1) the elasticity of Demand with respect to money, e_d, and (2) the elasticity of price with respect to Demand, e_p. Thus $e = e_p \cdot e_d$.

Book Six

Short Notes Suggested by the General Theory

CHAPTER 12

The Trade Cycle

In this chapter Keynes sets forth the view that the cycle is "mainly due to the way in which the marginal efficiency of capital fluctuates" (p. 313). Now the marginal efficiency of capital depends upon two things, (1) the series of prospective annual yields (that is, $R_1 + R_2 + \cdots + R_n$) from investment in a new capital good and (2) the cost of the capital good (that is, C_R). Fluctuations in the rate of investment are mainly due to changes in the R series and in C_R.

Contrast this with Gustav Cassel's view of the cycle. According to Cassel, cyclical fluctuations in the rate of investment are due to fluctuations in C_R, cost of capital goods, and in i, the rate of interest. The prospective yields (*i.e.*, the R series) he regarded as fairly stable since he inclined to the view that investment opportunities are limitless. But the *cost* of fixed capital goods were believed to rise more and more as the boom developed owing to a U-shaped supply curve and to the growing shortage of labor (migration from rural areas becoming exhausted). On the other hand, interest rates would tend to rise in the face of a rising demand for fixed capital goods. At higher rates of interest (despite relatively stable prospective yields) the capitalized *value* of new investment goods falls just at the moment when the *cost* of fixed capital goods rises. Now investment is a function of the margin between the *value* and *cost* of new capital goods. It is the narrowing of this margin, according to Cassel, that causes investment to fall at the end of a boom.

Keynes's analysis agrees with Cassel's with respect to the fluctuations in C_R. Also he agrees that, at times, a rising rate of interest "may certainly play an aggravating and, occasionally perhaps, an initiating part" (p. 315). But this, he suggests, is not typical. Instead, the primary and typically controlling factor is, he thinks, fluctuations in the prospective yields—the R series. This, together with fluctuations in C_R, accounts for the rise and fall in the marginal efficiency of capital. A sudden decline in the R series—the prospective annual yields from fixed capital goods—is the primary cause of the fall in the marginal efficiency of capital, though rising costs play a part. The explanation of the downturn is, then, "not primarily a rise in the rate of interest, but a sudden collapse in the marginal efficiency of capital" (p. 315).

Expectations of future yields (*i.e.*, the R series) rest in part on the abundance of capital goods in relation to other factors of production and in part upon the pessimism or optimism of entrepreneurs. Toward the end of a boom, excessive optimism may be strong enough to offset (1) the tendency toward diminishing marginal returns (the R series) due to the "growing abundance" of fixed capital goods, (2) the rising *cost* of capital goods, and (3) the rise in i, the rate of interest (p. 315). Reasonable estimates of the "future yields of capital-assets" are swept aside by an overoptimistic market.

It is improbable, says Keynes, that fluctuations in the marginal efficiency of capital are necessarily of a cyclical character (p. 314). Nevertheless, he suggests that there are "certain definite reasons" why "in the nineteenth-century environment, fluctuations in the marginal efficiency of capital should have had cyclical characteristics" (p. 314).

The reasons are as follows: As the boom progresses, "doubts suddenly arise concerning the reliability of the prospective yield" due to the decline in the *current* yield (that is, R_1) "as the stock of newly produced durable goods steadily increases"

(p. 317). At the same time the *current* costs of new capital goods rise. Thus the prevailing optimistic estimate of future yields of capital goods is increasingly displaced by disillusion. The collapse in the marginal efficiency of capital r, or the expected rate of return over cost, "precipitates a sharp increase in liquidity preference" (p. 316). This causes a rise in the rate of interest, and thus the situation is aggravated. But the initial factor is the decline in the marginal efficiency of capital. Liquidity preference increases *after* the collapse in r (p. 316). Moreover, the fall in r may also tend to cause a downward shift in the consumption function, especially for those who suffer losses in a declining stock market (p. 319).

The cyclical change in the expected "rate of return over cost" (Fisher) or the marginal efficiency of capital (Keynes) is thus grounded in (1) the inevitable decline in the prospective yields (the R series) as the large boom-time net additions to the stock of capital goods progressively creates a condition of capital saturation[1] and (2) the rising cost of new capital goods. But the cyclical swings in the marginal efficiency of capital are made more violent than the facts justify by "the uncontrollable and disobedient psychology of the business world" (p. 317). Keynes thus supports Alfred Marshall's stress on the role of confidence,[2] which, he thinks, economists have often underestimated and which "bankers and businessmen have been right in emphasizing" (p. 317).

The return of confidence takes time, and it relates to the "influences which govern the recovery of the marginal efficiency of capital" (p. 317). Herein lies the explanation of the time element or typical duration of the cycle. Expectations consist in part in volatile waves of pessimism and optimism,

[1] Investment may be carried beyond the point of saturation (which might be defined as just the right amount of capital) to the point of excess capacity.

[2] See my *Business Cycles and National Income*, W. W. Norton & Company, 1951, Chap 15.

but they are nontheless rooted in real factors which are not simply figments of the imagination. The time which must elapse before recovery begins, depends partly upon the magnitude of the *normal rate of growth of the economy* (p. 317) and partly upon the length of life of capital goods. The shorter the length of life of durable assets, the shorter the depression. And also, the more rapid the *rate of growth*, the shorter the depression (p. 318).

Moreover, with respect to inventories,[1] the duration of depression is influenced by the "carrying costs of surplus stocks." The decline of investment, income, and sales leads to an accumulation of undesired inventories the carrying costs of which "will seldom be less than 10 per cent per annum" (p. 318). The carrying costs are sufficiently high to speed the liquidation process.

Investment in "goods in process" necessarily is directly proportional to output. In the first phase of the downturn, inventory stocks rise (unintended investment), while goods in process decline. In the second phase, disinvestment occurs both in stocks *and* in goods in process. In the first phase of recovery of output, stocks may still be redundant, and so continued disinvestment in inventories may offset more or less the rise of goods in process. Eventually, as expansion progresses, both factors are favorable—entrepreneurs add to their inventory stock (intended investment) and goods in process increase along with rising output.

When the growth of the stock of real capital has reached its *appropriate* level, (end of investment boom) little further investment may be needed for some time. In this event capital

----

[1] In American usage (see Abramovitz, *Inventories and Business Cycles*, National Bureau of Economic Research, 1950) "inventories" includes (1) *stocks* of finished and unfinished goods and raw materials and (2) "goods in process." In Keynes's terminology the term "inventories" refers only to stocks, while "goods in process" is called working capital.

saturation has been reached, but not necessarily *excess* capacity. Still the investment spurt *is* likely to be overplayed, and so we may reach the condition of overinvestment (p. 320).

Overinvestment, however, may mean two things: (1) disappointed expectations in view of the ensuing unemployment; (2) genuine "full investment," *i.e.*, a condition in which the rate of return over cost is zero even under full employment.[1] In Keynes's view, it is, strictly speaking, only in the former sense that overinvestment has actually occurred in the past. Moreover, the illusions of the boom are likely to lead to *misdirected* investment—a clear waste of resources.[2]

Keynes considers the question of whether or not it is appropriate cycle policy to raise the rate of interest in a boom. He agrees that, if fundamental reforms cannot be instituted, a flexible interest rate may be better than nothing (footnote, p. 322), but of this he is not quite sure (p. 327). He urges that it would be desirable policy, not just to *level out* the cycle, but rather to perpetuate at least that measure of high employment reached in the boom. We have not had, he thinks, any recent boom "so strong that it led to full employment" (p. 322). A maintained low rate of interest would help to perpetuate a high employment level. In a correct state of expectation, the rate of interest in past booms has, in fact, been too high for full employment. But boom-time "over-

---

[1] For a fuller discussion of the "overinvestment" concept, see my *Business Cycles and National Income, op. cit.*, pp. 341–343.

[2] It must be emphasized that the basic explanation of the termination of a boom does not rest on illusions, misdirected investment, or "excess" investment. Keynes does indeed assert that five years of high investment in the United States prior to 1929 necessarily reduced the prospective yield of still *further* additions, "coolly considered" (p. 323). Yet the desired stock of capital goods might conceivably have been correctly appraised. The total net additions actually made might have been justified, but the *rate* of investment greatly exceeded the normal rate of growth. Accordingly, correct foresight would eventually require a sharp fall in the rate of investment.

optimism triumphs over a rate of interest which in a cooler light, would be seen to be excessive" (p. 322).

Keynes is, however, surely wrong when he suggests that the 1929 boom might have continued more or less indefinitely on a sound basis if a very low long-term interest-rate policy had been implemented (p. 323). Perhaps he only meant to say that it might have been *prolonged*. Yet considering the extraordinarily low yield on common stock and the consequent ease of getting money on highly favorable terms, it is even doubtful whether a lower rate of interest could, to any appreciable extent, have prolonged the boom.

The chapter ends with an ingenious discussion of Jevons's contribution to the trade cycle. According to Jevons, the trade cycle is caused by crop fluctuations due to rainfall cycles. Keynes argues that, at the time Jevons was writing, his explanation was extremely plausible. At that time, fluctuations in stocks of agricultural products must have been a major factor causing changes in the rate of investment. When crops are large, middlemen and storage concerns make large investments in the carry-over. Farmers' incomes rise as soon as the crops are sold to these concerns. Investment in these carry-over stocks raises total incomes. In the case of a poor harvest, however, the carry-over is small, and so investment in these stocks creates only a little income for farmers.

The point is that investment in agricultural stocks creates new income precisely as is the case with investment in fixed capital goods. Inventory investment is an important part of total investment and plays a significant role in the cycle. But investment in agricultural carry-over stocks is less important now than formerly.

Inventory investment in raw materials and semifinished and finished goods is usually the result of planned accumulations of stocks in response to expectations of increased sales or higher prices. Often, however, it is a result of unintended accumulation due to an unexpected decline in sales. And at times it is due to unavoidable excess carry-overs from large crops. The latter played perhaps a leading or even dominant role until around 1870.

The essentials of Keynes's discussion of the trade cycle can be summed up as follows:

1. The cycle consists primarily of fluctuations in the rate of investment.

2. Fluctuations in the rate of investment are caused mainly by fluctuations in the marginal efficiency of capital.

3. Fluctuations in the rate of interest have indeed at times played a significant role, but, more typically, changes in the liquidity preference schedule, induced by fluctuations in the marginal efficiency of capital, reinforce and supplement the primary factor (*i.e.*, changes in r).

4. Fluctuations in the marginal efficiency of capital, r, are due to (*a*) changes in the prospective yields (the R series) of capital goods and (*b*) changes in the replacement cost of capital goods C_R. Fluctuations in the cost of capital goods are due to changes in the rate at which investment is produced in a given period, in other words, to the extreme pressure placed upon the capital-goods industries during the boom. Fluctuations in costs are secondary and supplementary to the primary initiating factor, which is the fluctuation in the prospective yields of new capital goods.

5. Toward the end of a boom the decline in prospective yields on capital is due in the first instance to the growing abundance (and therefore lower marginal productivity) of capital goods. This is an *objective* fact, which in turn may induce a wave of pessimistic expectations (a psychological factor) so that the anticipated yield, once the turning point is past, is usually lower than the facts, coolly considered, justify.

6. In the absence of more thoroughgoing measures (*e.g.*, fiscal policy) a variable rate of interest may be useful as a

means to stabilize the cycle. Keynes, however, prefers a maintained low rate of interest in conjunction with other more radical measures designed to regularize the cycle.

7. Even boom-time levels of investment have typically failed to produce full employment. Thus in order to achieve sustained full employment it is not even enough to keep the boom going. Accordingly, Keynes did not believe it to be sound policy to choke off the boom. He was not impressed with the analysis which alleged that the depression is the inevitable consequence of the distortions of the boom. Any distortions that might exist could progressively be overcome by a program of sustained full employment. Merely to choke off the boom by an increase in the rate of interest "belongs to the species of remedy which cures the disease by killing the patient" (p. 323).

Keynes did not come to grips with the possible inflationary implications of a deliberate program of sustained full employment. Still more difficult are the maladjustments and distortions caused by wars and postwar restocking booms. Keynes, to be sure, was thinking, in this chapter, about normal peacetime conditions and not about the overfull employment of war and postwar booms.

CHAPTER 13

Notes on Early Economic Thinking and on Social Philosophy

[GENERAL THEORY, CHAPTERS 23, 24]

These chapters are brilliantly written and highly entertaining. Here Keynes lets himself go. Many would say that he threw caution to the winds and allowed his fancy to roam in an irresponsible manner.[1] Still, a careful reading will disclose the fact that, while flying his kite, he has his feet on the ground at least a good deal of the time! He wrote while the world was still at peace and one could daydream and speculate about Utopia. Things have changed.

All the elements of his theoretical system had already been expounded in earlier chapters, and these two concluding chapters add nothing of substance to the analytical arsenal in which we are primarily interested. But apart from his fasci-

---

[1] In connection with Keynes's sympathetic treatment of the mercantilists' emphasis on the desirability of a favorable balance and protectionist policy, it is only fair to remind the reader that his position is less extreme than has sometimes been suggested. Keynes noted that the mercantilists were often found opposing trade restrictions, that there are strong presumptions of a general character against trade restrictions, that the advantages of international division of labor are real and substantial, and that an immoderate protectionist policy "may lead to a senseless international competition for a favorable balance which injures all alike" (p. 338).

Moreover (p. 349), he explicitly argues for the "simultaneous pursuit" of high domestic employment "by all countries together" so as to restore "economic health and strength internationally" both in terms of high employment and of a large volume of international trade. This indeed was the program he sponsored at Bretton Woods.

215

nating flights of fancy, something can be gleaned from penetrating sidelights into his general system of thinking.

MERCANTILISM AND THE ROLE OF MONEY

The section on mercantilism harks back to the preoccupation of the *Treatise*—the role of money. The *General Theory* has the effect of relegating money to a place of less prominence than that assigned to it in the *Treatise*. Chapter 23 appears to be a reversion, in a measure, to his former enthusiasm concerning the importance of money.[1] The mercantilists are praised for the emphasis they placed on money. Home investment is governed (as they saw it) by the domestic rate of interest, and this in turn is governed by the quantity of money. The balance of trade is, they thought, rightly a chief concern of economic policy because, in the absence of domestic gold production, it controls a country's money supply. All this is a throwback to earlier views.

In the many quotations which he gives from the mercantilists, based on Heckscher, Keynes seems to give unqualified approval to a purely monetary theory of the rate of interest. Here and elsewhere he is not quite fair to his own system, which, taken in its entirety, is certainly not purely, or even mainly, monetary. In the complete Keynesian system the determinates of the rate of interest are not only the quantity of money and liquidity preference but also the investment-demand schedule and the consumption function (see Chap. 7 of this book). Here, perhaps even more than elsewhere, Keynes opens wide the door to the criticism that he is satisfied with a primitive and indefensible *monetary* theory of interest.

---

[1] Of course, I do not mean to imply that money is not highly important. But the role of money was overemphasized in the *Treatise*.

Some interesting brief comments on large issues are offered here and there. Thus it is suggested (footnote, p. 340) that all human history discloses, as we should expect from a knowledge of human nature, a long-run tendency for money wages to rise. Increasing wages, rising productivity, and a growing labor force could scarcely fail, more or less, to create a need for more money. "Thus, apart from progress and increasing population, a gradually increasing stock of money has proved imperative" in view of the tendency for the wage unit to rise over long periods of time.

The problems and actual experiences encountered in the mercantilist literature point, Keynes believed, to the conclusion "that there has been a chronic tendency throughout human history for the propensity to save to be stronger than the inducement to invest" (p. 347). He further suggests that the weakness of the inducement to invest may today lie in the extent of existing accumulations of capital goods, whereas in the mercantilist period the main explanation could perhaps be found in the great risks and hazards of that period (p. 348). Again on page 349 he refers to "the growth of wealth and the diminishing marginal propensity to consume."

Two points with respect to Keynes's statement are to be noted here, (1) that a large accumulated *stock* of capital tends per se to reduce investment opportunities, and (2) that the secular propensity to consume is falling.

With respect to the former it should be noted that the extent of future investment opportunities in any country depends partly on the degree to which capital accumulation has already been built up in relation to the prevailing technique and to the expanse and richness of its territory and resources, partly on the prospect of technological progress, and partly on population growth. The accumulation of a large stock of capital is indeed, as Keynes suggests, an important and relevant factor, but only one among several. The

year 1800 found England equipped with primitive tools; by
the end of the century she had accumulated a vast stock of
fixed capital. Thus nineteenth-century England is an example of the "exuberance of the greatest age of the inducement
to investment" (p. 353). With respect to the secular propensity
to consume, my own view has always been that it is reasonable
to assume it to be stable over time, as indeed Kuznets' data
appear to show.[1]

Keynes credits the mercantilists with fragments of practical
wisdom (p. 340) which later economists ignored. The "unrealistic abstractions of Ricardo" created a "cleavage between
the conclusions of economic theory and those of common
sense" (pp. 340, 350).

Chapter 23 ends with an appraisal of the strength and weakness of the analysis of saving, consumption, and investment
in Mandeville, Malthus, and Hobson. These views need no
comment here except to say that it is now possible, in view of
the theoretical system developed in the General Theory, to appraise the good and bad points in these authors in a manner
that was formerly not possible. One has only to contrast the
literature dealing with these writers prior to and after 1936
to see how inadequate the work of these forerunners was in
contrast with the theoretical structure erected by Keynes.

PRIVATE ENTERPRISE, THE WELFARE STATE, AND SOCIALISM

The issues raised in Chap. 23 are carried forward in Chap. 24
with special reference to the broader social implications of the
General Theory. Does the Keynesian analysis lead to socialism,
or is it a means of saving capitalism and individualism? Does
it lead to autarchy in trade, or to freer trade? Is "full employment" the goal, or is "full investment" the goal? Is main

[1] See pp. 75–78 in this book, and also Chap. 10 in my Business Cycles and
National Income, W. W. Norton & Company, 1951.

reliance to be placed on reducing the rate of interest, on raising the consumption function, or on enlarging the scope of public and private investment?

Merely to mention these issues is enough to show why the *General Theory* has aroused so much opposition. Keynes attacked dominant orthodox theories; he attacked conventional dogmas with respect to practical policy;[1] and he attacked the doctrine that reliance can be placed on automatic adjustment processes. He labeled as outstanding faults of the modern economy, failure to provide full employment and an inequitable distribution of wealth and income.

He contended that his analysis leads to directly opposite conclusions from those reached by orthodox economics with respect to the effect of measures (*e.g.*, taxation) designed to lessen the existing inequality of income. Greater equality will raise the consumption function; and an increase in the propensity to consume will serve to increase the inducement to invest[2] (p. 373). Yet he states, as part of his faith, a belief in the "social and psychological justification for significant inequalities of incomes and wealth," though not as large as those which existed in 1936 (p. 374).

[1] With respect to the two leading policy dogmas—the gold standard and the balanced budget—Keynes attacked the first directly but the second rather vaguely, though he stanchly supported loan expenditures as a means of raising Aggregate Demand. His earlier substitute for the gold standard was flexible exchanges, but later (Bretton Woods) his substitute was international machinery to permit exchange-rate adjustments and cooperation with respect to international investment and also with respect to domestic full-employment policies. With respect to a balanced budget, he did not hesitate to advocate loan expenditures, but he never faced up to the debt problem. After the First World War he advocated a capital levy, and in his pamphlet, *How to Pay for the War*, he still showed leanings toward this proposal. He never explored the implications of a growing public debt, the problems of debt management, or the important role of public debt as a means of providing adequate liquid assets in a growing economy.

[2] Without expressly saying so, this is one of the few instances in which Keynes in fact invokes the acceleration principle.

Similarly his analysis leads, he thought, to diametrically opposite conclusions from those reached by classical theory with respect to capital formation. According to the classicals, a high propensity to save is the source of high capital formation; and a high volume of saving was thought to be promoted by (1) a low propensity to consume and (2) a high rate of interest. As Keynes saw it, the opposite is true: a high level of investment is promoted by a low rate of interest and by a high propensity to consume. Basically, of course, the explanation for these different conclusions must be sought in the fact that the classicals were thinking of full-employment conditions, while Keynes had in mind the condition of underemployment.[1]

Keynes explicitly pointed out that a system of highly progressive taxes might reduce the net rate of return, after taxes, sufficiently to cause a low level of investment even though the rate of interest were low. "I must not be supposed to deny the possibility, or even the probability, of this outcome" (p. 377). Thus steeply progressive taxes might have the effect of preventing the optimum volume of capital formation. Here as so often in economics one encounters a dilemma: highly progressive taxes are favorable to a high level of consumption since such taxes promote greater equality of income, but they tend to have a deterrent effect on investment.

Keynes expressed forcibly the view that a program of continuous full employment would provide so high a rate of capital formation, assuming no radical change in the consumption function, that, within a generation or so, the marginal efficiency of capital would be driven down to zero (*i.e.*, the capital stock would increase until the condition of *full investment* is reached). Necessary conditions for this eventuality to occur would be (1) a fairly inelastic marginal efficiency

[1] The optimism of the classicals rested on the assumption of unlimited investment opportunities. On this basis, the higher the propensity to save, the greater the *amount* of capital formation.

schedule and (2) relatively small upward shifts in the schedule (*i.e.*, inadequate investment outlets due to a sluggish technology and a slow rate of population growth).

In line with his faith, often expressed, in the virtues of active enterprise (in contrast with the passive virtues of thrift) he unfurled the banner for the intelligence, determination, and executive skill of the entrepreneur (p. 376) while complacently foreseeing the gradual euthanasia of the *rentier* class.

He affirmed his faith in individual initiative and private enterprise. He was opposed to a system of state socialism. Nevertheless, the role of the State must, he thought, be greatly increased. "The State will have to exercise a guiding influence on the propensity to consume partly through its scheme of taxation, partly by fixing the rate of interest, and partly, perhaps, in other ways" (p. 378). Banking policy alone, via a low rate of interest, will not provide sufficient investment, he thought, for full employment. Public investment (but Keynes did not go into details) will be needed. Mixed companies— public authority combined with private initiative—have already played an important role in many countries, and such ventures may be expanded.[1] State control of investment in housing—low-cost public housing, lending, insurance, and guaranteeing operations—have become standard policies in all advanced countries. State action to ensure adequate investment, public and private, together with a tax policy designed to raise the consumption function—these are the types of measures which seemed promising. "It is not the ownership of the instruments of production which it is important for the State to assume" (p. 378). What is needed is "an adjustment between the propensity to consume and the inducement to invest" (p. 379). It is no more necessary, he thought, to socialize economic life now than formerly.

[1] The illustrations given in this and the sentence following are not drawn from Keynes.

Once sustained full employment is achieved, classical theory comes into its own. At full employment, the price system can be expected to direct productive resources, economically and wisely, into the right channels. What we suffer from is not misdirected employment but underemployment. The "free play of economic forces" can be trusted to give us efficient use of the factors of production (p. 379). In support of Keynes's position, one may cite the miraculous productivity and efficiency which the American economy has displayed ever since 1941 under the stimulus of a high level of Aggregate Demand.

Keynes was keenly aware of the advantages of individualism and free enterprise—the play of self-interest, the safeguard of personal liberty, the exercise of personal choice, and the variety of life which these institutions encourage. Indeed Keynes averred that he defended the enlargement of the functions of government (designed "to adjust the propensity to consume to the inducement to invest") as the "only practicable means of avoiding the destruction of existing economic forms" and promoting the "successful functioning of individual initiative" (p. 380). The world will not continue to tolerate unemployment. What is needed is a "right analysis . . . to cure the disease whilst preserving efficiency and freedom" (p. 381).

DID KEYNES CEASE TO BE A KEYNESIAN?

It has frequently of late been asserted that, toward the end of his life, the views of Keynes with respect to policy matters had substantially changed, indeed had reverted in large measure to the classical position.[1] That Keynes's theoretical

[1] A part of this section, with minor modifications, is taken from my chapter, Keynes on Economic Policy, in Harris, *The New Economics*, Alfred A. Knopf, Inc., 1947, pp. 203–207.

and policy conceptions would have developed along new lines, had he lived a decade or two longer, is highly probable. His was not a static mind. That his ideas would revert to the old conceptions is, however, more doubtful. Apart from hearsay, which is often conflicting and at best undependable, there is the interesting article, published after his death, in the June, 1946, issue of the *Economic Journal*.[1] This article, while dealing with the balance of payments of the United States, raises some larger issues with respect to the role of automatic forces and governmental intervention.

I have studied this article carefully, but I cannot find support for the thesis that it indicates a change in his fundamental thinking, let alone a "recantation," as has on occasion been suggested. Keynes always laid stress on the important role of automatic forces in economic life. Indeed, this could not be otherwise, since such State interventionism as he advocated (mainly in respect to monetary and fiscal policy) was designed to affect Aggregate Demand; beyond that, the automatic forces were assumed to be in control.

If we "succeed in establishing an aggregate volume of output corresponding to full employment as nearly as is practicable, *the classical theory comes into its own again* from this point onward" (p. 378, italics mine). Keynes was never an advocate of authoritarian government. In the *General Theory* he declared that his theory is "moderately conservative in its implications" (p. 377). No "obvious case is made out for a system of State Socialism which would embrace most of the economic life of the community" (p. 378). Again he sees "no reason to suppose that the existing system seriously misemploys the factors of production which are in use" (p. 379). There "will still remain a wide field for the exercise of private initiative and responsibility. Within this field the traditional advantages of indi-

[1] "The Balance of Payments of the United States," *Economic Journal*, June, 1946.

vidualism will still hold good" (p. 380). These advantages he details as those of "efficiency," "decentralization," and the "play of self-interest" (p. 380). The "reaction against the appeal to self-interest may have gone too far" (p. 380). Individualism is the "best safeguard of personal liberty" (p. 380). It is also the "best safeguard of the variety of life," the loss of which is the "greatest of all the losses of the homogeneous or totalitarian state" (p. 380). Individualism "preserves the traditions which embody the most secure and successful choices of former generations" (p. 380). Being the "handmaid of experiment as well as of tradition and of fancy, it is the most powerful instrument to better the future" (p. 380). "The authoritarian state systems of today seem to solve the problem of unemployment at the expense of efficiency and of freedom" (p. 381).

It is well to remember that these phrases are drawn not from the posthumous article but from the *General Theory* of 1936. Had they been written in 1946, many would have jumped at the conclusion that Keynes had "recanted."

In the article of 1946 he said similar things, but certainly no more in defense of individualism or the automatic forces than those I have cited above. The most telling phrases in this last publication are as follows (italics mine):

In the long run more fundamental forces may be at work, if all goes well, tending toward equilibrium. . . . I find myself moved, not for the first time, to remind contemporary economists that the classical teaching embodied some permanent truths of great significance, which we are liable today to overlook because *we associate them with other doctrines which we cannot now accept without much qualification.* There are in these matters deep undercurrents at work, natural forces, we can call them, or even the invisible hand, which are operating toward equilibrium. If this were not so we could not have got on even as well as we have for many decades past. . . . [1]

[1] *Ibid.*, p. 185.

I must not be misunderstood. *I do not suppose that the classical medicine will work by itself or that we can depend on it.* We need quicker and less painful aids of which exchange variation and overall import controls are the most important. . . . The great virtue of the Bretton Woods and Washington proposals, taken in conjunction, is that *they marry the use of the necessary expedients to the wholesome long-run doctrine.* It is for this reason that, speaking in the House of Lords, I claimed that "Here is an attempt to use *what we have learnt from modern experience and modern analysis,* not to defeat but to implement, the wisdom of Adam Smith."[1]

There is nothing in any of these statements which even approaches a recantation of the *General Theory*. Indeed the *General Theory*, as we have seen, contains similar statements in defense of individualism and the importance of automatic forces within the framework of a full employment economy.

Since the posthumous article in particular deals with international matters and especially with the joint effort, which Keynes did so much to implement, of the United States and Great Britain to restore multilateral trade to the utmost possible extent, something needs to be said about the alleged change, in later years, in Keynes's thinking along this particular line. Discussions with Keynes about monetary and financial matters, both in Washington and in London during the year 1941, disclosed that he was undergoing a pronounced shift in his attitude toward multilateral trade. This shift related, however, not to any fundamental change in his economic philosophy, but rather to what appeared feasible and realistic in terms of practical policy. Toward the end of 1941, Keynes at long last became convinced that the United States could be sufficiently relied upon to play a positive role in international economic and financial matters to justify risking a program of Anglo-American collaboration designed to promote a multilateral trading world. The isolationist tariff policy of the

[1] *Ibid.*, p. 186.

United States during the twenties had been superseded by the Hull trade agreements and the lend-lease program of President Roosevelt. Keynes had previously been profoundly impressed with the danger of being tied to the American economy. Witness the speculative and feverish foreign investments of the twenties, followed by a swift contraction of lending; the boom; and the "bust" in 1929, with its international repercussions. In this kind of world he was firmly convinced that Britain had better manage her balance of payments along "sterling-area" and "payments-agreements" lines, rather than risk the play of automatic forces in a multilateral world market subjected to violent and seemingly uncontrollable fluctuations.

But by the end of 1941 he became convinced that a new foundation, with Anglo-American cooperation, could be constructed upon which to erect a new multilateral trading world —or at least the thing was worth risking. On one occasion, in the autumn of 1941, when the importance of multilateral trade based upon high levels of employment in the advanced industrial countries and developmental programs in the more backward areas had been urged upon him in private conversation, his instant response was: "Well, on that basis we should all favor multilateral trade."

The above-cited declaration could scarcely be called a recantation. Already in 1936 in the *General Theory* he had said:

> But if nations can learn to provide themselves with full employment by their domestic policy . . . there need be no important economic forces calculated to set the interest of one country against that of its neighbors. . . . International trade would cease to be what it is, namely, a desperate expedient to maintain employment at home by forcing sales on foreign markets and restricting purchases . . . but a willing and unimpeded exchange of goods and services in conditions of mutual advantage (pp. 382–383).

This point of view he again reiterated in the *Economic Journal* article of 1946. A multilateral trading world is worth striving for. It cannot work without active international collaboration on the part of the United States. But, he declares (italics mine):[1]

> One is entitled to draw some provisional comfort from the present mood of the American Administration and, as I judge it, of the American people also, as embodied in the *Proposals for Consideration of an International Conference on Trade and Employment*. We have here sincere and thoroughgoing proposals, advanced on behalf of the United States, expressly *directed towards creating a system* which allows the classical medicine to do its work.

With respect to his attitude toward the United States in the thirties, to which I have referred above, it may be noted that he here refers to "this magnificent objective approach which a few years ago we should have regarded as offering incredible promise of a better scheme of things."[1]

There is no evidence here of any change in his fundamental economic thinking: what had changed was his view of the role of the United States in international economic affairs.[2] On the basis of the official program of the American government, a multilateral trading world could, he believed, succeed. But if the program is abandoned, or if for other reasons it fails, then "we, and everyone else, will try something different."[3]

---

[1] *Ibid.*

[2] An analogous case is the remark one frequently hears that Mr. A, who is an adherent of a compensatory fiscal policy, has changed his mind, because, forsooth, he advocated expansionist policies in the thirties, while in 1947 to 1952 he urged restraints upon public spending and a high tax policy! A man may wear an overcoat in winter and a straw hat in summer without being charged with inconsistency; but not so with respect to policy adaptations to changed economic conditions!

[3] Keynes, *Economic Journal*, June, 1946, p. 186.

In closing, Keynes raised quite frankly the question of whether or not his proposals may have "insufficient roots in the motives which govern the evolution of political society" (p. 383). He did not pretend to know the answer. Yet he offered his belief that, quite apart from the mood for bold ventures engendered by the devastating experiences of the interwar years, "the ideas of economists and political philosophers . . . are more powerful than is commonly understood" (p. 383). The power of vested interests, he thought, is exaggerated compared with the "gradual encroachment of ideas" (p. 383). Ideas, not vested interests, are, in the final analysis, "dangerous for good or evil" (p. 384).

OVERFULL EMPLOYMENT

Time has run fast since 1936. Had Keynes known how history was so soon to unfold itself, he might well have ended his book on a different note. The Second World War, of a magnitude hitherto undreamed of in terms of percentage of resources devoted to military uses, the vast postwar restocking and reconstruction boom, the cold war with its imperious defense budgets, the welfare demands of labor governments— all this ended for the time being any possibility of underemployment. The problem in most countries became rather that of overfull employment. In Britain, in the Scandinavian countries, in Holland, and elsewhere, governments greatly extended their control over economic life. Full employment was, however, primarily the result of the war and postwar developments, not of conscious policy. There was indeed always the fear that the backlogs of deferred demand and the vast defense and foreign-aid budgets in the United States would some day peter out, throwing the leading industrial country into depression. But in the labor and socialist governments of Europe at any rate there was the firm determination at all costs to maintain full employment and to raise consumption standards.

Not until 1952 did a weakening of demand in any major industry (*e.g.*, textiles) cause serious concern in England. Aggregate Demand remained high, but pockets of unemployment here and there began to appear. This was not the kind of problem envisaged by Keynes, nor indeed is it comparable in seriousness with the general problem of over-all inadequate demand. But it is nonetheless a knotty one. If it is sought to erase sectional unemployment merely by expansion of Aggregate Demand, the result is simply to cause an inflation. True, the maintenance of adequate, but not excessive, Aggregate Demand, aided by retraining and deliberate programs designed to relocate labor (with transportation allowances and housing at the new job sites) can surely do a great deal. But the human instinct is to "stay put," to bolster up declining industries, and not to undertake the hard task of promoting labor mobility.

For most advanced democratic countries, full employment has become a settled policy more quickly than Keynes had believed possible or indeed than would have been possible except for the war and its aftermath. Instead of unemployment, statesmen everywhere are confronted with inflationary pressures and the tough job of maintaining, within the pattern of full employment, a flexible economic system.

Keynesian critics may, however, have exaggerated the dangers of inflation and wage control in a full-employment society. The price inflation of 1946–1947 in the United States was a product of the war, not a test of peacetime full employment. Indeed from January, 1948, to December, 1948, the United States enjoyed full employment without inflation despite the absence of price and wage controls. The wholesale price level stood at 166 in January, 1948, and at only 162 in December, 1948, with an average of 165 for the whole year;

in January unemployment was only 2,065,00 and in December, 1,941,000, or 3.1 per cent of the labor force. When Beveridge suggested (*Full Employment in a Free Society*) the goal of only 3 per cent unemployment, there was a general disposition to ridicule the figure as utopian. Now, in fact, the goal of only 3 per cent is, everyone will agree, far more difficult for a country with high seasonal unemployment and rapid regional adjustments like the United States than for a small, compact, and homogeneous country like Great Britain. Nevertheless, the United States actually maintained this goal without price inflation and without controls during the year 1948. In 1949 and the first half of 1950, the inflationary pressure was eased, it is true, by a rise of unemployment to 5.5 per cent. But even this is considerably below the margin of safety suggested by some economists who have stressed the dangers of wage and price inflation in a full-employment society. Moreover, with unemployment averaging well below 3 per cent, wholesale prices fell from 116.5 (new index) to 109.7 during the two-year period from February, 1951, to January, 1953.

Had Keynes lived, we can be sure he would have critically reexamined his whole system of thinking.[1] His was not a mind that stood still. He was always in the vanguard, exploring new ideas and discarding old ones, even though these old ideas were his own. And in particular, he would no doubt have turned his attention to the practical problems of a full-employment society. As he himself said (p. 383) this would require "a volume of a different character . . . to indicate even in outline the practical measures in which they might be gradually clothed."

[1] For his last views on the rate of interest see p. 159 in this book.

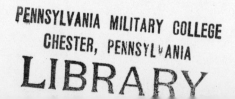

Index

231

DATE DUE

'JUL 0 7 1997		
~~DEC 0 2~~ 1997		
~~TN 100673~~		